Cambridge Elements

Elements in Criminology
edited by
David Weisburd
George Mason University, Virginia Hebrew University of Jerusalem

REVISITING JUSTICE

The Moral Meaning of Parole

Netanel Dagan
The Hebrew University of Jerusalem

Shaftesbury Road, Cambridge CB2 8EA, United Kingdom

One Liberty Plaza, 20th Floor, New York, NY 10006, USA

477 Williamstown Road, Port Melbourne, VIC 3207, Australia

314–321, 3rd Floor, Plot 3, Splendor Forum, Jasola District Centre,
New Delhi – 110025, India

103 Penang Road, #05–06/07, Visioncrest Commercial, Singapore 238467

Cambridge University Press is part of Cambridge University Press & Assessment,
a department of the University of Cambridge.

We share the University's mission to contribute to society through the pursuit of
education, learning and research at the highest international levels of excellence.

www.cambridge.org
Information on this title: www.cambridge.org/9781009587686

DOI: 10.1017/9781009587709

© Netanel Dagan 2025

This publication is in copyright. Subject to statutory exception and to the provisions
of relevant collective licensing agreements, no reproduction of any part may take
place without the written permission of Cambridge University Press & Assessment.

When citing this work, please include a reference to the DOI 10.1017/9781009587709

First published 2025

A catalogue record for this publication is available from the British Library

ISBN 978-1-009-58768-6 Hardback
ISBN 978-1-009-58772-3 Paperback
ISSN 2633-3341 (online)
ISSN 2633-3333 (print)

Cambridge University Press & Assessment has no responsibility for the persistence
or accuracy of URLs for external or third-party internet websites referred to in this
publication and does not guarantee that any content on such websites is, or will remain,
accurate or appropriate.

For EU product safety concerns, contact us at Calle de José Abascal, 56, 1°, 28003
Madrid, Spain, or email eugpsr@cambridge.org

Revisiting Justice

The Moral Meaning of Parole

Elements in Criminology

DOI: 10.1017/9781009587709
First published online: November 2025

Netanel Dagan
The Hebrew University of Jerusalem

Author for correspondence: Netanel Dagan, Netanel.Dagan@mail.huji.ac.il

Abstract: Expanding the boundaries of the "moral turn" in criminology to the realm of punishment administration, this Element proposes reconceptualizing parole through a moral lens. Drawing from a mixed-method study of parole hearings for homicide cases in Israel, the author argues that during parole hearings, parole actors (Attorney General representatives, secondary victims, parole applicants, and parole board members) conduct complex forms of moral labor, specifically retributive-oriented. This moral labor goes beyond rehabilitation and risk assessment to "do late justice." In doing such moral labor, parole actors negotiate the moral meaning of crime, character, and deserved punishment with the passage of time. In conclusion, as demonstrated by the current study, criminologists should engage to a greater extent with the moral meaning of punishment administration, and retributive theorists should aim to better understand the lived experiences of punishment.

Keywords: morality, parole decision-making, homicide, punishment administration, retributive justice

© Netanel Dagan 2025

ISBNs: 9781009587686 (HB), 9781009587723 (PB), 9781009587709 (OC)
ISSNs: 2633-3341 (online), 2633-3333 (print)

Contents

1 Introduction   1

2 Re-theorizing Parole   4

3 Context, Data, and Analysis   13

4 The Moral Landscape of Parole: Quantitative Findings   21

5 The Moral Theatre of Parole: Qualitative Findings   30

6 Revisiting Justice: Discussing the Moral Meaning of Parole   68

7 Conclusion   79

References   81

1 Introduction

The finality of crime presents an archetypal conundrum. Talmudic scholars, writing in late antiquity, told us that on the very first day of humanity, the first human beings had an existential crisis after committing their first sin and fearing its final consequences:

> The Sages taught: The day that Adam the first man was created, when the sun set upon him he said: "Woe is me, as because I sinned, the world is becoming dark around me, and the world will return to [the primordial state of] chaos and disorder. And this is the death that was sentenced upon me from Heaven." He spent all night fasting and crying, and Eve was crying opposite him. Once dawn broke, he said: "[Evidently, the sun sets and night arrives, and] this is the order of the world." He arose and sacrificed a bull whose horns preceded its hoofs.
> (Tractate Avodah-Zarah, 2020, p. 8a)

The ancient scholars invite us to reflect upon the nexus between crime and punishment through the lens of time. After their transgression, eating from the forbidden fruit, Adam and Eve experienced deep anxiety, loneliness, and a sense of fatality. They believed that the collapse of the natural order into chaotic darkness was the consequence of violating the divine law. They couldn't even comfort one other, weeping in their loneliness. However, they discovered that the passage of time was key to easing their despair; they realized that time in nature was not static or finite but dynamic and circular. The transformation from sunset to sunrise, each day renewed, brought not only natural change but also the human possibility for a second chance. Their amends, thus, were also a part of the natural order, symbolized by a bull that was divinely created.

A millennium and a half would pass from these Talmudic insights, and the relationship between time, crime, and punishment would become the heart of a then-innovative reformatory mechanism. In the nineteenth century, Norfolk Island (located east of Australia) was designated by the British Empire as a site for severe punishment (Morris, 2003). Against this backdrop, the penology of Alexander Maconochie, the governor of the Norfolk penal colony, stood in stark contrast. Inspired by religious ideas that coincided with Enlightenment ideas of humanism and crime prevention (Rotman, 2024), Maconochie criticized retributive "time sentences" for cruelly punishing past crimes, causing despair, and warping "judgement in forming estimates of moral character." Maconochie, later known as the "father of parole," proposed indeterminate rather than fixed punishments, divided into punitive and reformative training stages (in Moore, 2011, pp. 40–41). Release should be determined by earning "marks" through good conduct, education, and work. The goal of Maconochie's penology was thus to advance prisoners' "virtue" through "moral training" and the proper judgment of their "moral character" rather than to "avenge" (in Morris, 2003, p. xx). As can be seen, morality was a part of Maconochie's penology. Thus, the trajectory I suggest here – exploring the moral meaning of parole – merely re-energizes traces that are evident from parole in its earliest days.

Definitions of morality vary across and within disciplines such as philosophy, law, psychology, and sociology, and have been debated for centuries (Atari et al., 2023; Gert & Gert, 2025). Broadly defined, morality is an orientation toward understanding what is right and wrong, worthy and unworthy, and just and unjust, along with the interlocking sets of values, norms, and practices that are associated with them (e.g., fairness, proportionality) (Atari et al., 2023; Messner, 2012). Here I will focus primarily, but not exclusively, on the moral meaning of parole from a retributive perspective – a key sentencing theory that rests on moral intuitions of justice, fairness, and respect for the dignity and agency of offenders and their victims (von Hirsch, 2017). Retributivism has played a dominant role in punishment theory and policy-making over the past few decades (von Hirsch, 2017). Tadros (2011, p. 44), for example, noted that "retributivism is probably the most popular theory of punishment amongst those people working on the range of issues within the philosophy of criminal justice, and amongst criminal justice academics more generally."

Viewing parole through a moral lens aligns with the broader "moral turn" that criminology, an "ideal model for interdisciplinary science," has taken (Weisburd et al., 2025, p. 49). For centuries philosophy has posed questions directly relevant to criminological concerns. However, with some exceptions (Bottoms & Jacobs, 2023; Messner, 2012; Millie, 2016), criminology and philosophy both in research and teaching have usually been viewed as distinct, and perhaps unrelated, subjects (Arrigo & Williams, 2006). Criminologists, for their part, have long called for legal philosophers to focus less on abstract moral principles and more on actual lived moral experiences in society, warning philosophers against imposing "repressive measures" based on philosophers' "beliefs" (Durkheim, 1893/1997, p. 172) (Durkheim, 1920/1973, pp. 110–111). However, despite the increasing criminological attention to moral themes (Bottoms & Jacobs, 2023), moral analysis is often seen as distant from broader social structures that criminologists typically study. Criminologists still tend to overlook the valuable analytical insights that moral analysis can offer for theorizing and studying crime and punishment (Bottoms & Jacobs, 2023; Messner, 2012).

In recent years, there has been a "glimmer of a moral awakening" in criminology (Messner, 2012, p. 7). Criminologists are increasingly called upon to engage with moral and normative inquiries, as criminology inevitably involves an analysis of social values and normative choices, and thus "all criminologists have to be interested in morality" (Bottoms, 2002, p. 24). The call for "philosophical criminology" (Millie, 2016) aims to connect criminology more deeply with the moral emotions, judgments, and values of criminal justice system (CJS) actors, their relatives, and society at large. Such an approach suggests that morality is shaped by practice, and people are motivated, implicitly and explicitly, by personal, social, political, and institutional moral positions (Ievins & Williams, 2025). This moral turn, however, is only in its formative stages in criminological research (Arrigo & Williams, 2006; Bottoms & Jacobs, 2023; Lanskey et al., 2023).

Recent examples of criminological analysis from a moral perspective are perception-choice processes in criminal behavior (Messner, 2012), the role of morality in disabling the perception of crime as a viable alternative (Brauer & Tittle, 2017), the emotional burdens experienced by offenders for violating their own moral values (Griffin et al., 2019), and the moral trajectories of penal communication (Schinkel, 2014), rehabilitation, recovery, and desistance for offenders (Jang & Johnson, 2024; Maruna & Mann, 2006).

I would argue that this "moral turn" holds particular importance for studying the ostensibly utilitarian, bureaucratic, and managerial work of punishment administration. Specifically, I would suggest that there is a need to explore the moral meaning of parole. Sentencing and parole decision-making for long-term prisoners (particularly lifers) have serious moral meaning. Denying the realistic possibility of release from prison deprives offenders of the "most basic liberties without giving hope of restoration," rendering their punishment so severe that it shares "some characteristics with death sentences" (*Graham v. Florida*, 2010, pp. 69–70).

Despite being cast as "god-like" to prisoners (Palacios, 1994), having a dramatic impact on prisoners' (and their relatives') lives and the safety of victims and society at large (Vîlcică, 2018), the work of parole boards is "notoriously understudied" (Young & Pearlman, 2022, p. 783) because parole hearings are "notoriously difficult to access" (Young & Chimowitz, 2022, p. 238). Exploring the moral meaning of parole could stir up key retributivist premises regarding the finality of punishment. Such an analysis could also shed light on the role of parole in revisiting the morality of crime, character, and punishment.

Parole decision-making is often viewed as both "bureaucratic" (Guiney, 2023, p. 627) and "highly routine and automatic" (Proctor, 1999, p. 213). Although scholars point to some moral themes of parole in various contexts (Aviram, 2020; Dagan, 2023, 2024; Hawkins, 1983; Vîlcică, 2018; Young & Chimowitz, 2022), a full review of the moral meaning of parole has yet to be conducted. To address this gap, through a mixed-method analysis of parole hearings for long-term prisoners (N= 483) convicted of homicide, I seek to shed light on parole's neglected moral meaning, with a focus on the moral labor of parole actors throughout the hearings. I argue that parole actors – Attorney General Representatives (AGRs), secondary victims (SVs) such as victims' parents or children, parole applicants, and parole board members – engage during the hearings in multiple forms of *narrative moral labor* (Maruna & Liem, 2021; Warr, 2019). Such moral labor refers to the process of creating moral and identity-related narratives under the complex organizational pressures and incentives of parole hearings.

I would argue that through parole hearings, parole actors move well beyond narrow risk or rehabilitation assessment. Instead, they conduct various forms of moral labor to manage the meaning of character, crime, and deserved punishment. As our quantitative findings indicate, retributive factors make a unique contribution to the accumulative variability accounted for in a board's decision-making. Furthermore, our qualitative analyses support the idea that a board's interpretation of factors associated with character, crime, and punishment can result in "doing late justice," revisiting the justice and morality of the sentencing court. The perspective I suggest here calls for criminologists to engage to a greater extent with the moral meaning of punishment administration and for retributive theorists to better understand the real experiences of punishment.

2 Re-theorizing Parole

2.1 Parole as a Moral Puzzle

Modern CJSs create a division of labor between sentencing courts and punishment administration authorities, such as prisons, parole boards, or community supervision agencies (in the United States, "corrections"). Sentencing and punishment administration are typically governed by distinctive legal frameworks (criminal versus public law), decision-makers (judges versus administrative experts), penal orientations (retributive versus utilitarian), and levels of visibility (public versus closed-door proceedings). In addition, sentencing and punishment administration are shaped by different institutional objectives, sources of legitimacy, and interpretations of what punishment is and should be (Garland, 2011; Kerr, 2019).

One key distinction between sentencing and punishment administration emerges from their different penological orientation. Many Western jurisdictions, including several in the United States, England and Wales, Sweden, Canada, and Israel have adopted a retributive orientation at sentencing, at least to some extent (Roberts & Gazal-Ayal, 2013). Traditional retributivists seek to hold offenders accountable through proportionate punishment according to the severity of their crimes, regardless of possible beneficial consequences (e.g., crime prevention) (von Hirsch, 2017). For such retributivists, punishment should deliver censure to the offender correspondent with the crime's seriousness at the time of its commission. Thus, retributive sentencing is primarily backward-looking, and its validity is assessed at the moment of sentencing (von Hirsch, 2017). In contrast, the work of punishment administration authorities is often viewed as utilitarian, bureaucratic, and largely detached from a moral assessment (Garland, 2001; Kerr, 2019). Such punishment administration work focuses on future-looking rehabilitation and risk prevention, operating within a dynamic time frame that considers the offender's past criminal history, present status, and future developments (Laub & Sampson, 2003).

A key authority in punishment administration is the parole board. One of the primary ways prisoners obtain release from prison is through parole boards and similar bodies that exercise enormous power in determining imprisonment length (Rhine et al., 2017). Parole is considered a primary feature of a positivistic-utilitarian philosophy which seeks to maximize social utility through rehabilitation and risk reduction. Accordingly, parole board members aim to identify biological, psychological, and social factors that underlie crime, and can order conditional release from prison before the prescribed prison term has been completely fulfilled (Petersilia, 2003; Reitz, 2017; Simon, 1993).

Parole has also become a central part of theoretical accounts that emphasize the declining interest of modern CJSs in retributive ideals (Simon, 1993). Feeley and Simon (1992, p. 452), for example, described how the rise of the "new penology" involves the "replacement of a moral ... description of the individual with an actuarial language that is managerial, not transformative." Garland (2001, p. 127) similarly argued that with the rise of a "culture of control," crime is viewed as a routine risk to be avoided and managed rather than as a "moral aberration that needs to be specially explained." Whereas scholars have identified a disconnect between formal actuarial-risk CJS policies envisioned by the "new penology" and the real work of field-level parole actors (which is more clinical, subjective, and moral-oriented) (Hannah-Moffat, 1999; Lynch, 1998; Maurutto & Hannah-Moffat, 2006), parole scholarship and policy-making are usually firmly located within the theoretical framework of utilitarian risk and rehabilitation (Petersilia, 2003; Simon, 1993).

Parole presents a moral puzzle for retributivists, considering its utilitarian, future-oriented, risk-based, and expert-driven nature (von Hirsch & Hanrahan, 1978). One might recall Kant's (1798/1999, p. 138) infamous "categorical imperative" – a central moral philosophical concept which resists "a theory of happiness looking for some advantage to be gained by releasing the criminal from punishment." Parole, from its formative stages in the nineteenth century, was viewed as a "scandal" and "outrage" (Rotman, 2024, p. 17). Later, during the 1970s, parole, particularly in indeterminate sentencing jurisdictions, was criticized for undermining justice and fairness (von Hirsch & Hanrahan, 1978).

Traditional retributivists view crime severity as crystallized at the time of the crime, remaining static and unchanged (von Hirsch, 2017). As one court put it: "The 'just deserts' and other determinate aspects of punishment have been unyieldingly fixed in the original sentence" (*Ezeh & Connors v. U.K.*, 2003). Thus, retributivists view any post-crime rehabilitation, amends, or the collateral effects of the punishment as extraneous to determining the deserved sentence, as they are unrelated to harm and culpability at the time of the crime (von Hirsch, 2017). On these grounds, retributivists have often blamed parole for its immorality, stressing that sentencing "is bound by a set of moral values" and thus is in conflict with the risk-oriented parole process that is "value-free" (Brodeur, 1990, p. 508; Rubin, 2003, p. 58). Parole has been described by such retributivists as "unjust" (von Hirsch & Hanrahan, 1978, p. 1), as it "undercuts deserved punishment" (Robinson, 2012, p. 144) and negates "society's interest in retribution" (*Skipper v. South Carolina*, 1986, p. 14). Retributivists have also blamed parole for creating symbolic sentences (Nagel, 1990) and "coddling criminals and victimizing law-abiding citizens" (Larkin, 2013, p. 313). In addition, retributive scholars have criticized parole for creating disparate sentencing, based on a "synthesis of record facts and personal observation" (*Greenholtz v. Inmates of Nebraska*, 1979, p. 10), and allowing parole for "whatever reason, whatever facts, for however long" (Ball, 2009, p. 944). Such broad decision-making has been blamed for shaving decades off prison time in a quick decision, operating outside public view, with minimal judicial scrutiny (Rhine et al., 2017).

Criminologists have questioned parole's utility, claiming that supervised early release from prison has little to no crime-prevention value (Reitz & Rhine, 2020; Shute, 2004; Solomon et al., 2005; Travis, 2005) and suffers from poor public support, especially regarding the parole of violent or recidivist prisoners (Fitzgerald et al., 2023; Roberts et al., 2000). Although there have been attempts to morally revive parole as a "final equalizer" of punishment (von Hirsch & Hanrahan, 1978), or to allow punishment decisions to be made with "cooler heads" (Morris, 1974), or to better reflect society's evolving sentiments toward crime (The Sentencing Project, 2024), these efforts have been largely unsuccessful, leading scholars and policymakers to advocate for the abolition of parole or its restriction through parole guidelines (e.g., "truth in sentencing" laws) (Petersilia, 2003). More recently, the Model Penal Code's drafters argued that in an ideal system, parole would be abolished, as parole boards are inferior to courts in determining proportionality (ALI, 2017).

However, parole remains a resilient institution and is not expected to disappear anytime soon (Rhine et al., 2017); it is often described as a "phoenix" rather than a "corpse" (Larkin, 2013). Several U.S. jurisdictions, Australia, Canada, England, and Wales view parole as an efficient crime reduction mechanism and as promoting reintegration; in murder cases, life with parole is a common sentence in several jurisdictions, including in the United States (Kleinstuber & Coldsmith, 2020; Seeds, 2022; Reitz & Rhine, 2020). Parole has also been justified less openly for controlling prison overcrowding or incentivizing prison discipline (Petersilia, 2003; Simon, 1993). In Europe, parole is rooted in prisoners' rights to re-socialization, dignity, and liberty (van zyl Smit & Corda, 2018). All European jurisdictions use parole, at least for certain groups of prisoners (van zyl Smit & Corda, 2018). Despite the utilitarian focus of parole scholarship, developments in penal theory and criminology invite its exploration through a retributive lens.

2.2 Penal Theory: Individualizing Retribution

Penal theorists have increasingly pushed the boundaries of retributive justice to incorporate more fully post-crime developments as part of a more holistic moral assessment of offenders. The aim of this shift is to individualize retributive theory, moving from a focus on crime to character, from penal quantity to quality, from monologue to dialogue, and from a philosophical to an empirical desert.

Regarding *from crime to character*, traditional retributivists, as discussed, view the core normative justification for punishment as a moral desert for a crime at the time of its commission (von Hirsch, 2017). However, a more holistic vision of retribution argues that offenders' desert should be assessed not only on the basis of their crime but also on their overall moral character (Murphy & Hampton, 1988). From this perspective, crimes arise within the broader context of an individual's life, situated within temporal, social, and historical circumstances (Smith, 2016). Thus, just as pre-crime factors (e.g., criminal history) provide insight into an offender's character, post-crime developments (e.g., remorse) should also influence the assessment of the "totality" of offenders' moral character – sometimes even mitigating their culpability or harm caused – and hence their deserved punishment (Roberts, 2008; Smith, 2016). From this viewpoint, truly repentant and morally reformed individuals who have turned their lives around should not be treated in the same way as individuals who remain hardened and unrepentant (Murphy, 2012). Moral character is also increasingly important for policymakers. The U.S. Supreme Court holds that life sentences without parole for juveniles are unconstitutional as they mean the "denial of hope; it means that good behavior and character improvement are immaterial" (*Graham v. Florida*, 2010; *Miller v. Alabama*, 2012). The European Court of Human Rights holds that whole life sentences mean that prisoners "can never atone for [their] offence" and ignore the "capacity to change" (*Vinter v. U.K.*, 2013; *Matiošaitis & Others v. Lithuania*, 2017), and that parole should promote "morally desirable 'good behaviour'" (*Ezeh & Connors v. U.K.*, 2003).

Regarding *from penal quantity to quality*, traditional retributivists calibrate the severity of punishment using quantitative time units of liberty deprivation (e.g., months, years) (von Hirsch, 2017). This quantitative assessment is objective, determined by the degree to which liberty deprivation interferes with an offender's interests based on typical "living standards" (von Hirsch, 2017), and "disembodied" from the offender's physical experience (Garland, 2011, p. 768). In contrast, criminologists have long empirically found that the "pains of imprisonment" extend far beyond the deprivation of liberty per se (Hulley et al., 2016). However, only recently have retributivists begun to engage seriously with the implications of the "subjective" (e.g., old age) and "objective" (e.g., solitary confinement) prison experience (Kolber, 2009) or the collateral consequences of punishment as part of the retributive agenda (Hoskins, 2014). This emerging subjectivism of retributive theory has been further reinforced by critiques of sentencing decisions, which are often made with only a superficial understanding of prison realities (Hanan, 2020). Even traditional retributive theorists are increasingly accepting the role of "quasi-desert" factors – the passage of time, old age and infirmity, or efforts to right the wrong – as possibly mitigating the level of deserved punishment even if they are unrelated to harm and culpability (von Hirsch & Ashworth, 2005).

Regarding *from monologue to dialogue*, traditional retributivists view the censure delivered by a court as a one-sided message (von Hirsch, 2017). This perspective frames censure as not only focusing on the crime's severity but also on the offender's future, encouraging offenders to engage with "secular penance," moral reform, and reconciliation with the community as a response to their censure (Duff, 2001). Theorists maintain that although offenders are morally expected to respond to their punishments, such responses should not alter the deserved level of punishment (von Hirsch & Ashworth, 2005). More recently, theorists have gone further, viewing censure as part of a two-sided dialogue and thus as a dynamic (or responsive) rather than static concept (Duff, 2001; Maslen, 2015; Roberts & Maslen, 2014). Thus, offenders' response to censure after sentencing (e.g., the extent to which they internalize the original sentencing censure) should be considered in determining the level of punishment. Indeed, these theorists suggest that by ignoring offenders' positive moral responses, a troubling message is sent – namely, that their responsiveness, atonement, and respect for community norms are irrelevant (Dagan & Roberts, 2019; Roberts & Maslen, 2014).

Finally, regarding *from philosophical to empirical desert*, moral philosophers are seen as the primary arbiters of justice, using their "transcendent" judgments, analysis, and reasoning. In contrast, the "empirical desert" approach shifts the focus to how ordinary people perceive justice, suggesting that punishments that deviate from lay intuitions of justice can undermine the public's willingness to comply with the law (Robinson & Holcomb, 2021). Specifically, scholars argue that the wide use of life-without-parole sentences would conflict with community views of justice, undermining the moral credibility of criminal law; as such, these sentences should be seriously limited (Robinson, 2012).

In this study I will draw upon these theoretical developments, which individualize retributivism, to analyze parole hearings. I will thus define *retributive theory* broadly as consisting of different theoretical strands that have in common the idea that it is intrinsically (deontologically) good for wrongdoers to receive punishment for their wrongful acts. This broad retributive perspective will be contrasted with the utilitarian theory, the aim of which is to increase overall net social welfare by preventing crime through deterrence, incapacitation, or rehabilitation (von Hirsch, 2017).

2.3 Criminology: The Reality of Out-of-Court Morality

The increasing individualization of retribution can be contextualized alongside a parallel yet unrelated shift, still only in its formative stages, in criminological scholarship toward examining the moral labor done outside courts (Ievins, 2023; Schinkel, 2014; Warr, 2019). As part of this turn, criminologists are directing greater empirical attention to the moral dimensions of prison experiences and rehabilitation practices both in prison and in community settings.

First, criminologists are increasingly interested in the *moral dimensions of rehabilitation and desistance from crime*. Concepts such as "moral rehabilitation," "moral improvement," or "moral reform" (McNeill, 2012) propose a "thicker" rehabilitative theory (Rotman, 2024). Such a rehabilitation approach synthesizes retributive and utilitarian ideas for promoting offenders' dignity and civic status (du Bois-Pedain, 2024). This rehabilitative approach emphasizes responsibility-taking, moral reform, and harm mitigation rather than focusing narrowly on reducing re-offending (Jang & Johnson, 2024; Liem & Richardson, 2014; McNeill, 2012). Restorative justice scholars, in a related field (but from a different theoretical motivation), have emphasized several moral themes such as righting the wrong, rebalancing the harm caused, responsibility, and censure internalization, all of which are oriented toward reconciliation and making amends (Daly & Proietti-Scifoni, 2011).

Second, criminologists are increasingly recognizing the importance of analyzing *prison reality through the lens of retributive theory*. Scholars have aimed to expand the empirical inquiry into subjects such as respect and fairness (Tyler, 2010), dignity (Snacken, 2021), and liberty in prisons (Van Ginneken & Hayes, 2017). Scholars have also expanded the analysis of the "pains of imprisonment" literature to the unique physical and psychological pains of life sentences (or other lengthy prison terms), with a special focus on aging and dying processes in prison (Seeds, 2022). Specifically, criminologists have suggested that "courts do not have a monopoly on moral communication" (Ievins, 2023, p. 182). Qualitative scholarship shows that moral-related processes such as guilt internalization (Ievins, 2023; Schinkel, 2014), managing the "moral weight" of crime (Dagan & Rennie, 2025), moral reflection and transformation, splitting the self (Jarman, 2020), and developing a sense of agency and law-abiding self (Crewe et al., 2020; Liem & Richardson, 2014) are key for prison and reentry experiences. They have also suggested that "people in prison make excellent philosophers, for reasons related to what they are deprived of" (Liebling, 2021, p. 104). This emerging literature encourages examining empirically the moral meaning of parole.

2.4 Changing the Lens: Toward Parole Hearings as a Moral Forum

The *quantitative literature*, mostly from the United States, shows an overall low violent recidivism rate for those paroled after a life sentence; nevertheless, the parole prospects for such individuals are generally low (Durose et al., 2014; Ostermann, 2015; Kleinstuber & Coldsmith, 2020; Nellis & Bishop, 2021). The quantitative literature has highlighted the overall contribution of punitive parole decision-making to mass incarceration through parole denial or revocation of release (Lin et al., 2010). In terms of parole decision predictors, studies have highlighted the strong role of crime severity (Caplan, 2007; Caplan & Kinnevy, 2010; Efodi, 2014; Huebner & Bynum, 2006; Morgan & Smith, 2005; Vîlcică, 2018), victim impact statements (VISs) or public position (Morgan & Smith, 2005; Roberts, 2008), and/or negative prosecutor recommendations (Murcia, 2022; Young & Pearlman, 2022). Some studies have shown crime severity to be the most influential factor, followed by crime type, criminal history, number and age of victims, institutional behavior, mental illness, applicant's age and gender, respectively (Bowman & Ely, 2017; Caplan,

2007; Huebner & Bynum, 2006; Kinnevy & Caplan, 2008). Scholars have highlighted utilitarian factors, such as institutional misconduct (Caplan, 2007; Mooney & Daffern, 2014), recommendations from corrections staff (Morgan & Smith, 2005), risk assessment (Mooney & Daffern, 2014), and mental health (Houser et al., 2019) as the factors commonly given the most weight. Studies have also revealed, however, that crime severity (Matejkowski et al., 2011), VISs (Caplan, 2010; Hail-Jares, 2021), or time served (Vîlcică, 2018) are not reliable predictors of parole outcomes. The relationship between the expression of remorse, self-reflection, or "insight" and parole release is also inconsistent across studies (Dalke, 2023; Vîlcică, 2018; Walk & Dagan, 2024; Young et al., 2016). Current parole prediction scholarship suffers from limitations, as the same factors are not consistently examined across studies, for legal (e.g., whether there is a minimum time required before parole eligibility) (Caplan, 2007) or methodological reasons, thus leading to inconsistent findings (Mooney & Daffern, 2014). Also, moral themes have rarely been treated as a distinct subject of study in the criminological quantitative literature.

The *qualitative literature* reveals that some parole board members in the United States (Ruhland, 2020) and Europe (Dagan, 2023; Griffin, 2018) hold both retributive and utilitarian philosophies. Studies on parole decision-making both in the United States and other jurisdictions reveal that parole boards frequently use their discretion to effectively "re-sentence" prisoners by denying parole for reasons tied to retribution and general deterrence (Annison & Guiney, 2022; Aviram, 2020; Dagan, 2023; Rhine et al., 2017; Shammas, 2019). Parole decision-makers have also been found to overemphasize crime severity and future risk rather than focusing on post-release reentry and rehabilitation (Houser et al., 2019; Padfield et al., 2000) and to consider rehabilitation only after punishment has been exhausted (Rieger & Serin, 2024). In addition, parole decision-making has been linked to punishing prisoners for their evil character (Hawkins, 1983), re-stigmatizing them for their past crimes (Herbert, 2024; Pogrebin et al., 2015), or morally educating them to be responsible agents (Padfield et al., 2000). Parole boards, often collaborating with prosecutors and victims, have also been found to preserve the "moral memory" of the crime during the hearings (Aviram, 2020; Dagan, 2023) and appease punitive populist media, politicians, and the public by demonstrating a "tough-on-crime" approach (Annison & Guiney, 2022; Fitzgerald et al., 2023). Remorse and demonstrations of "insight" into the crime are often perceived by parole boards as evidence of prisoners' moral transformation, their ability to recognize the cause of their criminal behavior within their identity, and their willingness to view the CJS's authority as legitimate (Dalke, 2023; Young & Chimowitz, 2022).

Parole applicants' moral labor during hearings and how this labor shapes the meaning of parole, however, remain under-researched, particularly when compared to the extensive empirical research on the moral dimensions of sentencing (von Hirsch, 2017). The little research that does exist indicates that parole applicants experience parole hearings as a liminal space – an intermediate phase that oscillates between stages such as death and rebirth, hope and disappointment, preparation and suspension, self-improvement and self-assessment (Aviram, 2020; Werth, 2017). During hearings, parole applicants attempt to mitigate their responsibility for past crimes and to present themselves morally (Lavin-Loucks, 2002). During their post-release period, parolees have been found to view themselves as ethical agents, either as individuals who were always moral or who underwent a moral reform (Liem & Richardson, 2014; Werth, 2017).

The current criminological literature highlights the value of examining parole hearings through a moral lens. However, the moral potential of parole still remains largely unfulfilled, particularly in the sensitive and under-researched context of homicides (Brookman, 2015). First, as noted, the current literature has rarely focused on parole's moral meaning. To my knowledge, no study has analyzed or juxtaposed the moral contributions of all parole actors or the moral dynamics at play during hearings. Second, recent moral analyses of parole, as illustrated, have tended to adopt a predominantly pessimistic perspective, emphasizing the punitiveness of parole decision-making. Criminologists often view retributivism as synonymous with "eye-for-an-eye" emotive vengeance (Andrews & Bonta, 2014). In contrast, penal theorists usually view retribution as a *limit* on penal severity based on the principle of proportionality (von Hirsch, 2017).

Criminologists' rather pessimistic view of retribution seems to distance them from the retributive meaning of parole, leading them to overlook key questions: What role does retributivism, broadly defined, play outside the courtroom, within parole hearings for homicide cases? Specifically: (1) How does retributivism evolve between sentencing and parole, and what implications does this evolution have for parole decision-making? (2) How do different parole actors view and engage with the morality of parole during hearings? and (3) What is the relative weight of retributive factors compared to risk and rehabilitation in parole decision-making?

Based on the current literature, I hypothesize that within the utilitarian risk-oriented arena of parole, moral discourses will not lie at the heart of parole discourses; instead, the focus will be on the classic role played by risk and rehabilitation assessment (Caplan, 2007; Feeley & Simon, 1992; Garland, 2001; Mooney & Daffern, 2014). The moral labor of parole actors will be limited, at best, to punitive parole rejection in serious cases (Aviram, 2020; Dagan, 2022; Hawkins, 1983; Rhine et al., 2017) or the management of specific parole factors (e.g., remorse, crime denial) (Lavin-Loucks, 2002; Young & Chimowitz, 2022). However, based on a mixed-method analysis of parole hearings for homicide cases in Israel, I will also suggest that parole hearings involve a rich, complex, and multidimensional moral labor undertaken by parole actors, aside from their traditional risk and rehabilitation assessment. I will argue that such moral labor is conducted by parole actors by using their own "voice," by "co-authoring" their narrative with other actors, or in response to other actors' narratives (Maruna & Liem, 2021). As part of this moral labor, parole actors will revisit the morality of character, crime, and punishment. Thus, the approach I suggest here invites criminologists to more seriously consider morality as a framework for analyzing parole, specifically, and the work of punishment administration, generally.

3 Context, Data, and Analysis

3.1 Context

In the following section, I will provide an overview of the Israeli parole system, which exemplifies a relatively common discretionary model of parole, similar to several discretionary parole jurisdictions in Europe and the United States (Padfield et al., 2010; van zyl Smit & Appleton, 2019). To enhance the generalizability of the analysis, I will highlight key similarities and differences between the Israeli parole system and that of major Western jurisdictions.

3.1.1 The Parole Framework in Israel

The Israeli penal system, derived from English law (Sharon, 2003),[1] uses proportionality as its "guiding principle" (s.40). Rather than using strict sentencing guidelines, as is common in U.S. jurisdictions, Israeli sentencing courts consider, based on their discretion, the severity of the crime to determine the deserved sentencing range. Rehabilitation and risk factors, meanwhile, are used to determine specific sentences within this range or to justify deviations (Roberts & Gazal-Ayal, 2013).

---

[1] In England and Wales, murder, carrying a mandatory life sentence, is defined as intentional killing. A "whole life order," without the possibility of parole, is the starting point for the minimum term for very serious murder cases (the starting point for the minimum term for less serious murder ranges from 15 to 30 years). Manslaughter, carrying up to a maximum of life imprisonment (sentencing range: 1–24 years), is defined as intentional killing but where a partial defense applies, among other cases (Martin, 2024).

At the time relevant to this study, the legal definition of "murder," similar to that of several other jurisdictions, was "caus[ing] the death of any person with premeditation" (ss.300(a)(2)-301(a) (pre-2019 reform). In line with other common law jurisdictions, the specific *reasons* for the murder are usually irrelevant to the conviction. Furthermore, spontaneous intention, even formed in the "blink of an eye" (*Jaber v. State*, 2017, par. 11), is considered as much of an intention as one formed through lengthy deliberation (Ashworth & Horder, 2013). Exceptions aside, the sentence for murder (at the time relevant to this study) was a *mandatory indeterminate life sentence* (ss.300-301; pre-2019 reform), similar to the sentence in Canada, England and Wales, and several U.S. jurisdictions (van zyl Smit & Appleton, 2019). However, unlike these jurisdictions, sentencing judges in Israel do not determine a minimum time to be served before parole eligibility.[2] Again, at the time relevant to this study, manslaughter – an unlawful cause of an individual's death – carried a discretionary maximum sentence of twenty years' imprisonment (s.298; pre-2019 reform).

After sentencing, as in some other jurisdictions (van zyl Smit & Appleton, 2019), a commutation committee may recommend to Israel's president the mitigation of the indeterminate life sentence to a determinate life sentence of at least thirty years (terror-related murder is excluded from parole) (Counter-Terrorism Act, 2016). Commutation committee recommendations are typically laconic, issued without oral hearings, and unpublished (ss.29–30). The commuted determinate sentence becomes the maximum sentence to be served and is subject to the possibility of parole.

As is common in the United States (Rhine et al., 2017) and Europe (Padfield et al., 2010), parole in Israel is considered a privilege rather than a right and is subject to the board's "very wide" discretion (*State v. Ganame et al.*, 2009). Similar to the United States (Reitz, 2017) and England and Wales (Beard, 2023), judicial intervention in the board's decisions is reserved for exceptional cases involving unreasonableness, illegality, or other public law grounds (*Stazenko v. State*, 2018). In contrast to U.S. parole jurisdictions, which are governed by the executive branch (Hritz, 2021, p. 17), the Israeli parole board is a "quasi-judicial body" and its decision-making "should align with the criminal law's purposes" (*Doe v. Israel*, 2022, par.21). However, the board "should not again look at punishment considerations, as it is a sitting instead of a sentencing court" (*PCATI v. Parole Board*, 2001).[3]

---

[2] In England and Wales, sentencing courts specify a minimum term to be served before parole eligibility based on "crime seriousness" ("tariff"). After the "tariff," a continued detention is decided by a parole board based on "dangerousness."

[3] In England and Wales, the board is "court-like," containing both adversarial and inquisitorial elements (Padfield et al., 2022). Parole members come from a variety of professional backgrounds

The board operates under the Parole Law 2001 and conducts oral hearings for every eligible case in the presence of the parties (s.16). The board's panels may change on a rotating basis, but the same panel is generally expected to hear the case in future hearings. In terms of parole decision-makers, there are ninety-four chairpersons (judges), almost all (96%) being Jewish (Gov, 2025). Applicants must request their release to initiate a parole procedure (Parole Procedures, 2025, s.3). Parole decisions for lifers are handled by a special parole board, whereas other eligible prisoners are assessed by a regular board. Both types of boards consist of three voting members: a chairperson (who is a judge) and two experts in criminology, psychology, or social work. An Israel Prison Service (IPS) officer participates without voting rights (ss.32–33). Both types of boards will hereafter be referred to collectively as *"the board."*

The first parole eligibility point typically occurs after two-thirds of an original *determinate* sentence has been served (after being commuted) (s.5); for lifers, this point usually occurs at least twenty years after sentencing (ss.29–30). In case of parole denial, a subsequent hearing can be scheduled within a year (or six months for other prisoners) or when new circumstances arise (s.19). With some exceptions, parole hearings are conducted within prison walls. These hearings include the presence of the applicants, their counsel, the AGRs, and often the SVs who are permitted to voice their arguments (s.16). If parole is granted, the board imposes license conditions until the end of the sentence, which can be revoked if the applicants violate their conditions (s.13). After the hearing, the board announces its decision, or takes other procedural steps (e.g., invites reports) (Sharon, 2003).

In common with other discretionary parole jurisdictions, the main criterion when deciding on release is *public safety* (Padfield et al., 2022; Rhine et al., 2017).[4] The board must focus on *risk and rehabilitation*, assessing whether "the prisoner deserves to be released and that his release does not endanger the safety of the public" (ss.3–5).[5] Parole jurisprudence reinforces this agenda, stating that the board shall consider two aspects: "the potential risk to the public . . . and the prisoner's rehabilitation prospects" (*PCATI v. Parole Board*, 2001). To this end, the board may consider, based on its wide discretion, and similar to other discretionary parole jurisdictions (Kokkalera & Allison, 2024; Padfield et al.,

---

(e.g., judges, psychologists) (Beard, 2023). In the United States, board members typically have professional and educational backgrounds in law, criminology, social work, or psychology. Typically, the board has some adversarial elements but is not considered a court (Bing, 2011).

[4] In England and Wales, the board shifted from focusing on "early release" of determinate sentence prisoners to focusing on the "delayed release" of those who have served their "tariff" risk test for all eligible prisoners (Padfield et al., 2022). U.S. parole laws often have specific risk requirements for sex offenders' parole (Rhine et al., 2017).

[5] This could be read with the legislation of risk-oriented legislation toward sex offenders restricting their return to the victims' environment (2004) and supervising them in the community (2006) (Aviram, 2021).

2022), crime severity, criminal history, risk assessment, prison behavior, correctional treatment, attitude toward rehabilitation and work, post-release plans, VISs, and reports from the prison rehabilitation authority (PRA), police, probation, or prison officers. The board may also consider personal factors such as age and family status (s.9). Special risk assessments are required for cases involving domestic violence, sex crimes, or mental health issues (ss.11–12). For lifers, the board must consider whether the applicants have "notably and tangibly changed in terms of understanding the severity of [their] actions," and their willingness to integrate within and contribute to society (s.10(b)). Additionally, "in cases of special severity and circumstances," for all crimes, the board may consider whether the prisoner's release "will severely harm the public's trust in the justice system" or "general deterrence," or will result in "an unreasonable disparity between the severity of the offense ... and the term which the prisoner will actually serve" (s.10(a)).[6]

Beyond the board members, the following are the key actors in the hearings:[7] (a) parole applicants, who are legally represented by private or public counsel during the hearing.[8] If applicants refuse to attend the hearing, the prison warden must explain the implications of their decision (Parole Procedures, 2025); (b) the Attorney General, who is represented by public prosecutors. These AGRs handle parole work in addition to their ordinary prosecution work. However, the AGRs are generally expected to assume that retribution has been addressed in sentencing and focus instead on risk (State Attorney, 2018);[9] (c) victims of violent or sex crimes (or their surviving family members, SVs), who can submit written VISs regarding the "expected risk from the release" (Rights of Victims of Crime Law, 2001, s.19).[10]

---

[6] Several U.S. jurisdictions allow parole denial based on crime severity, whether the release will "depreciate the seriousness of his crime as to undermine respect for law," the "sufficiency" of the amount of time served, or "the existence of adverse public concern or notoriety" (Rhine et al., 2017). In California, however, the core inquiry in parole hearings is "current dangerousness" rather than "heinousness of the crime" (*In re Shaputis*, 2011). In England and Wales, the board has "no role or involvement in the punitive element of a sentence" and parole is linked to current risk (Parole Board, 2022, p. 6).

[7] Aside from ad-hoc correctional officers, or applicants' family members who rarely testify in the hearings.

[8] However, some U.S. jurisdictions exclude applicants from legal representation at the hearings (e.g., New York State Parole Handbook, 2010).

[9] In England and Wales, the Secretary of State representative is a prison or probation officer, and in rare cases legal counsel; they work mainly to help the board navigate the evidence and provide a view of the prisoner's risk (Beard, 2023).

[10] U.S. jurisdictions allow VISs at parole hearings; many of them also allow victims to make parole recommendations (Rhine et al., 2017). In England and Wales, the victims generally can attend the hearing and even challenge the board's decision through the Secretary of State (Padfield et al., 2022).

3.1.2 Parole in Israel: Empirical Evidence

In 2018, the total number of "criminal" prisoners in Israel was 6,119. This population included 369 lifers, 510 sentenced for more than twenty years, 325 sentenced for fifteen to twenty years, and 441 sentenced for ten to fifteen years (IPS, 2018). Official data on parole in Israel are limited and confusing, particularly for long-term prisoners (Rosenfeld & Noah, 2021). The overall parole rate in 2016 for violent crimes was about 23%, compared to about 28% for all crimes. Those who served full sentences were almost twice as likely to recidivate as those who were paroled (25% versus 44.3%), with the lowest recidivism rates observed among those sentenced to more than ten years (22.8%) (Ouaknine & Ben-Zvi, 2021). The low parole rate in Israel has been criticized by scholars, both for contributing to the severe overcrowding in Israeli prisons and for failing to exhaust the contribution of supervised release to crime prevention (Efodi, 2014; Gazal-Ayal & Marzuk-Maklada, 2023).

A study of the board's decisions and the PRA's recommendations from 2015 for short-term prisoners ($N = 306$; release rate: 46%; M = 2.5 years) revealed that the PRA recommendations were more strongly based on rehabilitation, whereas the board appeared to give similar weight to rehabilitation and risk, and crime severity predicted only the board's decisions (Walk & Dagan, 2024). Rosenfeld & Noah (2021) explored a sample of 2017–2018 cases ($N = 346$; $M = 2$ years) and found that parole rejection was associated with insufficient rehabilitation and crime severity, whereas release was linked to young age, first incarceration, and short sentence. This study also identified a large proportion of applicants (36%) who relinquished their opportunity to seek parole by not applying or withdrawing their application later. The AGRs were found to be highly resistant to parole in both short and long-term cases (Dagan, 2023 ($N = 130$); Rosenfeld & Noah, 2021 ($N = 346$)). Finally, Ouaknine et al. (2021) examined short-term prisoners released in 2017–2018 ($N = 5,076$; $M = 2$ years) and found the parole release rate to be 32%, with the board decision-making heavily relying on rehabilitation and education. However, they found no significant impact of parole on recidivism during the first year of release.

3.2 Data, Sample, and Analysis

Written parole decisions provide a means to understand how release decisions are justified (Rivera-Laugalis et al., 2024). Researching parole decisions is a complex task, given the nuanced moral discourses raised by parole actors during the hearings – including judicial, disciplinary, clinical, and risk data (Ruhland, 2020). The textual density, richness, and complexity of parole hearings are unsurprising; indeed, the word parole in French means "*word* of honor"

(Petersilia, 2003), implying the narrative-oriented meaning of this mechanism. To gain both depth and breadth in analyzing parole hearings, in this study I combine a quantitative analysis of parole decision-making with a qualitative analysis of parole actors' experiences, which together form the complex phenomenon of parole, and integrate the findings into a cohesive picture.

3.2.1 Data

To analyze the moral meaning of parole, I focus on murder and manslaughter parole cases (collectively, "homicide cases"). Typically, the stakes are high in homicide cases, due to the severity of the crimes and punishments, and the hearings are morally charged, thorough, and involve more significant SV participation. However, the two groups differ in some respects (e.g., level of blame, sentence severity, legal requirements), allowing for an exploration of any qualitative or quantitative variation (Kazemian & Travis, 2015; Levitt, 2021).

Israel's PRA is officially responsible by law to rehabilitate ex-prisoners in Israel (PRA, 2022). The database includes all board hearings for murder and manslaughter cases archived by the PRA during a five-year period from 2018 (when the PRA began archiving its work) to 2022, inclusive. Access to this database was ethically approved by the PRA and by Hebrew University's institutional review board. The data comprise 483 transcripts of parole hearings (hereinafter also, *cases*): (a) 229 murder cases (in such cases, prisoners are referred to as "lifers") and (b) 254 manslaughter cases. These cases involved a total of 304 applicants (118 applicants having more than one hearing).[11] Each hearing produced on average between five and fifteen transcribed protocol pages, recorded verbatim by the board's clerk, yielding about 4,000 pages of protocols.

3.2.2 Sample

The moral meaning of parole, particularly the board's retributive orientation, emerges from its decisions to grant or reject parole applications. Therefore, it is important to understand the applicants' characteristics, their (commuted) determinate sentences, and their parole timelines. Table 1 presents the background and imprisonment characteristics of the 304 applicants, as they derived from the 483 parole decisions.[12]

---

[11] In addition, sixty-eight cases were of *post-release* supervision hearings (e.g., managing license conditions) (see Section 5.4.4.)

[12] Seven applicants served their sentence for fatal negligence. They were omitted from the analysis for the different severity of their sentences ($M = 2$ years, $SD = 1.3$, $MED = 1$) and narrative patterns.

Table 1 Descriptive statistics for all parole applicants

Characteristics	Decisions of All Prisoners ($N = 483$)	Prevalence/Mean Decisions of Murder Cases (Lifers) ($N = 229$)	Decisions of Manslaughter Cases ($N = 254$)
Male	94.0%	93.4%	94.5%
Married	54.6%	55.1%	53.8%
Jewish[13]	55.3%	69.0%	42.9%
First incarceration	63%	58.2%	65.6%
Granted parole release	33.3%[14]	26.2%	39.8%
Sentence length (in years, after commutation)	$M = 21.9$ ($SD = 10.2$), $MED = 20.0$	$M = 30.9$ ($SD = 5.7$), $MED = 30.0$	$M = 13.7$ ($SD = 5.5$), $MED = 14.0$
Age (at the hearing)	$M = 46.1$ ($SD = 13.5$), $MED = 44.0$	$M = 55.1$ ($SD = 11.5$), $MED = 55.0$	$M = 38.1$ ($SD = 9.5$), $MED = 37.0$

As Table 1 shows, the board's authority spanned a substantial period of prison time, averaging about ten years for murder cases and approximately 4.5 years for manslaughter cases. The sentence length for all lifers (after commutation) was severe, with an average of about thirty-one years ($M = 30.9$, $SD = 5.7$, $MED = 30.0$), which was significantly longer than for all manslaughter cases ($M = 13.7$, $SD = 5.5$, $MED = 14.0$). Furthermore, in terms of release rates, lifers had a substantially lower release rate (26.2%) than did manslaughter offenders (39.8%). A chi-square test confirmed that this difference in release rates was statistically significant ($\chi2(1) = 10.025$, $p = 0.002$).

A key function of the board is to determine to whom early release should be granted and at what point. Table 2 presents the descriptive statistics of 160 parole applicants who were *released*. Among those released by the board, lifers were released after serving a longer percentage of their sentence compared to prisoners convicted of manslaughter – 77.3% (22.8/29.5 years on average) versus 74.4%

---

[13] The non-Jewish group were mostly Arab-Muslim (43.5%), and a very few Druze (2.2%) – all Israeli citizens.
[14] The non-release decisions include both rejection ($N = 142$) and delaying the case for further hearings ($N = (178)$) for further risk assessment or missing reports (Palmor Report, 2010).

Table 2 Descriptive statistics of released parole applicants (N = 160)

Characteristics	Prevalence/Mean		
	Decisions of All Released Prisoners (*N* = 160)	Decisions of Murder Cases (Lifers) (*N* = 60)	Decisions of Manslaughter Cases (*N* = 100)
Male	93.8%	91.7%	95.0%
Female	6.3%	8.3%	5.0%
Married	52.7%	62.1%	42.3%
Jewish	45.6%	61.7%	36.0%
First incarceration	69.7%	66.7%	70.6%
Sentence length (in years, after commutation)	M = 19.1 (SD = 9.8), MED = 18.0	M = 29.5 (SD = 5.6), MED = 30.0	M = 12.9 (SD = 5.6), MED = 13.0
Time served (at release)	M = 13.6 (SD = 7.9), MED = 13	M = 22.8 (SD = 6.2), MED = 23.0	M = 9.6 (SD = 4.4), MED = 10.0
Age (at hearing)	M = 43.2 (SD = 12.3), MED = 42.0	M = 53.4 (SD = 10.3), MED = 53.0	M = 37.5 (SD = 9.3), MED = 36.5

(9.6/12.9 years on average). However, a Mann-Whitney U test revealed that this difference was not statistically significant ($U = 1295.500$, $p = 0.251$).

3.2.3 Methods

Quantitative Content Analysis

To determine the extent to which moral considerations influenced parole decisions (0 = denial, 1 = release), a quantitative-inductive content analysis (Krippendorff, 2018) of the categories appearing in the cases was conducted in three stages: (1) *establishing content categories*. I analyzed fifty cases (equally divided between murder and manslaughter) to establish content categories. Thirty categories were identified in this process: fifteen positive (e.g., "admits guilt" or "actively participates in prison treatment"), twelve negative (e.g. "severe crime," "disciplinary misconduct," "insufficient treatment"), and three additional categories representing the positions of the AGRs, the SVs, and the police; (2) *Coding*. Three law/criminology students coded the cases according to the categories identified in the previous stage. In cases of disagreement, discussions were held until a consensus was reached. I also reviewed and confirmed the students' coding: (3) *grouping categories into factors*. Based on criminological and penal theory literature, the categories were conceptually divided into four groups: *utilitarian factors* consisting of (a) *risk and rehabilitation*, and *retributive factors* consisting of (b) *crime-related*, (c) *moral character-related*, and (d) *punishment-related* factors.[15]

Qualitative Content Analysis

To achieve a rich description of the narratives involved in parole hearings, I conducted an in-depth qualitative analysis of the hearings for all parole actors and utilized inductive-oriented thematic coding of the transcripts (Charmaz, 2006). I focused on the conceptual and relational meaning of narratives that emerged from the meaning of whole sentences rather than individual words (Elo et al., 2014). As in similar qualitative studies of parole decision-making (Appleton, 2010; Ruhland, 2020; Young & Chimowitz, 2022), the transcripts were thoroughly read three times to identify connections, associations, and preliminary interpretations. Similar statements were coded and grouped into categories. To enhance transferability, I aimed to provide a "thick" description of the hearings, including rich examples (translated by a bilingual translator); contextualize the analysis; conceptualize the findings at a more abstract level; and acknowledge the study's limitations (Charmaz, 2006). To preserve anonymity, all personal details about the actors were omitted in reporting the findings.

4 The Moral Landscape of Parole: Quantitative Findings

To understand the scope of the moral labor conducted by the board, compared to its risk and rehabilitation assessment, the frequency of each parole category, as well as its association and effect size with the board's decision, was analyzed. Table 3 shows the prevalence of utilitarian and retributive categories and factors in the board's decisions.[16] Each category was coded as binary: "1" if present in the board's decision and "0" if absent. A Bonferroni correction was applied to account for the potential inflation of Type I errors due to multiple tests. With thirty tests performed, the significance threshold was set at $p = 0.00167$. Results with p-values below this threshold were considered statistically significant and are marked with a star. Uncorrected p-values are reported in parentheses. The phi coefficient (Φ), which is reported in Table 3, is a measure of the association

---

[15] Some of these categories could be labeled "quasi-desert" (von Hirsch & Ashworth, 2005).
[16] Differences in category prevalence between murder and manslaughter cases were also examined, and no substantial variance was observed.

Table 3 Prevalence of categories and factors in parole board decisions (N = 483) and their association and effect size with parole outcomes

Category/Factor	Prevalence in Parole Board's Decision (%)	Chi-Square[17] (uncorrected p-value)	Phi Coefficient (Φ)
Utilitarian factors (risk/rehabilitation)			
Participation in prison treatment	61.5%	$\chi^2 = 49.885$* ($p < 0.001$)	0.323
Post-release rehabilitation program	43.8%	$\chi^2 = 42.029$* ($p < 0.001$)	0.296
Participation in prison education/work	39.5%	$\chi^2 = 26.289$* ($p < 0.001$)	0.234
Motivation for treatment	36.7%	$\chi^2 = 14.354$* ($p < 0.001$)	0.173
First incarceration	30.1%	$\chi^2 = 8.624$ ($p = 0.003$)	0.134
Medium-high risk assessment	28.8%	$\chi^2 = 6.358$ ($p = 0.012$)	−0.115
AGR's position	27.8%	$\chi^2 = 35.053$* ($p < 0.001$)	0.271
Victim's position	22.0%	$\chi^2 = 7.800$ ($p = 0.005$)	0.128
Insufficient treatment	19.1%	$\chi^2 = 45.774$* ($p < 0.001$)	−0.309
Prison misconduct	17.2%	$\chi^2 = 10.155$* ($p = 0.001$)	−0.146
Police's position	12.7%	$\chi^2 = 18.061$* ($p < 0.001$)	0.194
Negative prison intelligence[18]	12.4%	$\chi^2 = 7.002$ ($p = 0.008$)	−0.121
Current mental health condition	8.1%	$\chi^2 = 1.486$ ($p = 0.223$)	−0.056
Supportive family	7.3%	$\chi^2 = 9.566$ ($p = 0.002$)	0.141
Drug involvement	4.6%	$\chi^2 = 4.050$ ($p = 0.044$)	−0.092

---

[17] Significance is determined based on a Bonferroni-corrected threshold of $p < 0.00167$. Results meeting this threshold are marked with a star.

[18] Intelligence information received from intelligence sources and related to the applicant's prison behavior (e.g., fights in prison), for the board's eyes only.

Table 3 (cont.)

Category/Factor	Prevalence in Parole Board's Decision (%)	Chi-Square (uncorrected p-value)	Phi Coefficient (Φ)
Recidivist	4.1%	χ2 = 0.662 (p = 0.416)	−0.037
Impulsivity	3.3%	χ2 = 1.598 (p = 0.206)	−0.058
Prior parole release	3.3%	χ2 = 0.034 (p = 0.853)	−0.008
Crime-related factors			
Especially severe crime	20.5%	χ2 = 20.102* (p < 0.001)	0.205
Harm to public trust in CJS or general deterrence	6.2%	χ2 = 4.030 (p = 0.045)	−0.092
Moral character-related factors			
Admits crime	43.4%	χ2 = 31.844* (p < 0.001)	0.258
Expresses remorse	42.5%	χ2 = 25.664* (p < 0.001)	0.231
Change in understanding the seriousness of actions ("insight")	29.9%	χ2 = 76.195* (p < 0.001)	0.399
Criminal record	14.1%	χ2 = 2.515 (p = 0.113)	−0.072
Special role in prison	13.3%	χ2 = 8.819 (p = 0.003)	0.136
Victim compensation	12.2%	χ2 = 14.058* (p < 0.001)	0.171
Apology to victim	10.2%	χ2 = 14.905* (p < 0.001)	0.176
Plea bargain	8.5%	χ2 = 3.374 (p = 0.066)	0.084
Punishment-related factors			
Severe medical condition	6.0%	χ2 = 3.624 (p = 0.057)	−0.087
Insufficient time served	5.2%	χ2 = 0.080 (p = 0.777)	0.013

between two binary variables. It provides an effect size indicating the strength of the relationship between each category and the board's decision.

As Table 3 shows, key categories related to *utilitarian factors* (risk and rehabilitation) were highly prevalent and significantly associated with parole decisions. "Participation in prison treatment" was highly prevalent and moderately and significantly associated with parole decisions (61.5% prevalence; $p < 0.001$, Phi coefficient= 0.323). Similarly, "post-release rehabilitation program" was prevalent and was significantly associated with parole decision (43.8% prevalence; $p < 0.001$, Phi coefficient = 0.296), indicating a weak to moderate association with parole outcome. Categories with weaker but still significant associations with parole decisions included "participation in prison education/work" (39.5%, $p < 0.001$, Phi coefficient= 0.234) and "motivation for treatment" (36.7%, $p < 0.001$, Phi coefficient= 0.173).

The second factors were *retributive-oriented* and consisted of three groups: (a) *Crime-related factors*. Among these, "especially severe crime" emerged as the most prevalent category (20.5%) and showed a significant though weak association with parole decisions ($p < 0.001$, Phi coefficient = 0.205). (b) *Moral character-related factors*. "Admitting the crime" showed a significant though weak relationship with the board's decision (43.4% prevalence; $p < 0.001$, Phi coefficient= 0.258). "Expressing remorse" was similarly influential, with a significant and weak association with parole decisions (42.5% prevalence; $p < 0.001$, Phi coefficient= 0.231). Additionally, a "change in understanding the seriousness of actions" was highly prevalent and exhibited a significant and moderate association with parole decisions (29.9%; $p < 0.001$, Phi coefficient= 0.399). (c) *Punishment-related factors* showed no association with parole decisions.

After examining the categories considered by the board and their respective prevalence, it was important to assess the weight that different groups of factors and individual categories carried in influencing parole decisions. Understanding the relative impact of these factors, particularly retributive factors, provides deeper insight into the moral meaning of parole decision-making. As such, a hierarchical multiple logistic regression analysis was conducted to examine the relationship between multiple sets of independent variables and the binary dependent variable – the decision to grant or deny parole. In this approach, used previously in research in the context of parole decision-making (Houser et al., 2019; Huebner & Bynum, 2008), factors are entered in steps, allowing for a systematic assessment of how each group of factors contributes to parole decisions, as well as the unique effect of individual independent variables. Hierarchical multiple logistic regression is appropriate here because it enables us to isolate the contribution of each set of factors while controlling for previously entered factors (Cohen et al., 2013). The following section outlines the methodology used to group the variables according to their respective factors.

As mentioned, following the identification of relevant categories related to parole decisions, these were grouped into four conceptual factors.[19] Subsequently, all thirty categories were systematically evaluated for their statistical significance with the dependent variable, effect size, and prevalence. During this process and based on its results, twelve categories (e.g., "prior parole release," "impulsivity") were excluded from further analysis.[20] The remaining eighteen categories were then assessed for multicollinearity. For instance, although conceptually distinct, several categories primarily reflected the perceived risk posed by the prisoner (e.g., "medium-high risk," "prison misconduct").[21] The final set included eight categories[22] and three additional variables[23] predictive of parole decisions, which were organized into four blocks and entered sequentially. These blocks represented sociodemographic variables and three key groups of factors influencing parole decisions: utilitarian, crime-related, and moral character-related. Table 4 presents the results of the hierarchical multiple logistic regression analysis.

In Model A, which included control variables (ethnicity and age),[24] the variability accounted for was relatively small (Nagelkerke R^2= 0.045, $\chi^2(2)$= 14.046, $p < 0.001$), suggesting that demographic factors alone accounted for only 4.5% of the variability in parole decisions. In Model B, utilitarian factors such as "risk assessment" or "participation in prison treatment" were added, significantly increasing the variability accounted for to 25.9% (Nagelkerke R^2= 0.259, $\chi^2(3)$= 74.209, $p < 0.001$). In Model C, crime-related factors such as

---

[19] Although factor analysis could have been used to group variables, it was not conducted due to an insufficient number of observations for each variable to ensure the stability and reliability of the analysis. Instead, variables were grouped on the basis of theoretical considerations as described earlier.

[20] Special role in prison, harm to public trust in CJS or general deterrence, medium-high risk assessment, and criminal record did not meet the Bonferroni-corrected threshold in the chi-square tests. However, they were still retained in the analysis due to their theoretical relevance in explaining parole outcomes, as supported by the study's conceptual framework.

[21] Categories with a variance inflation factor (VIF) exceeding 5.0 were considered multicollinear, and in such cases, the category with the strongest association with parole decisions or the highest prevalence was retained.

[22] Medium-high risk assessment, participation in prison treatment, post-release rehabilitation program, harm to public trust in CJS or general deterrence if released, change in understanding the seriousness of actions ("insight"), special role in prison, compensation, and criminal record.

[23] Ethnicity (non-Jewish), age at the hearing, and length of sentence (after commutation).

[24] Gender was omitted as a control variable due to the relatively small number of decisions regarding female prisoners, resulting in statistical insignificance; however, these decisions were still retained in the analysis to ensure comprehensive representation and consistency with subsequent qualitative analysis.

Table 4 Hierarchical multiple logistic regression models of parole board release decisions (N= 429)

	Model A (Sociodemographic variables)	Model B (Utilitarian factors)	Model C (Crime-related factors)	Model D (Moral character-related factors)
Constant	0.087	−1.526	−1.536	−1.533
Ethnicity (non-Jewish)	0.397 [1.487]	0.405 [1.499]	0.392 [1.480]	0.300 [1.350]
Age at the hearing	−0.022* [0.979]	−0.013 [0.987]	0.007 [1.007]	0.008 [1.008]
Medium-high risk assessment		−1.098*** [0.334]	−1.043*** [0.352]	−1.160*** [0.313]
Participation in prison treatment		1.540*** [4.665]	1.519*** [4.567]	1.276*** [3.583]
Post-release rehabilitation program		0.903*** [2.467]	1.045*** [2.844]	0.733** [2.082]
Length of sentence (after commutation)			−0.042** [0.959]	−0.042* [0.959]
Harm to public trust in CJS or general deterrence if released			−1.527** [0.217]	−1.635** [0.195]
Change in understanding the seriousness of actions ("insight")				1.349*** [3.852]
Special role in prison				0.172 [1.187]
Compensation				0.115 [1.122]
Criminal record				−0.902* [0.406]
−2 Log likelihood	527.830	453.621	438.511	407.135
Block χ2	14.046***	74.209***	15.109***	31.376***
Nagelkerke R^2	0.045	0.259	0.299	0.376

Notes: Odds ratios are provided in brackets.
* $p < 0.05$; ** $p < 0.01$; *** $p < 0.001$.

"length of sentence" or "harm to public trust" were introduced, raising the variability accounted for to 29.9% (Nagelkerke R^2= 0.299, $\chi^2(2)$= 15.109, $p < 0.001$). Finally, in Model D, moral character-related factors such as "change in understanding the seriousness of actions" and "compensation" were added, further improving the model fit and increasing the variability accounted for to 37.6% (Nagelkerke R^2= .376, $\chi^2(3)$= 31.376, $p < 0.001$). The final model accounts for 37.6% of the variability in parole decisions, reflecting the combined influence of *demographic*, *utilitarian*, *crime-related*, and *moral-character-related* factors.

Model D provides the most comprehensive explanation of the factors influencing the board's decisions. Regarding utilitarian factors, applicants classified as medium-to-high risk were approximately 68.7% less likely to be released than not released (OR= 0.313, $p < 0.001$). The presence of a post-release rehabilitation program emerged as another significant predictor of parole (OR= 2.082, $p < 0.01$), with applicants who planned to participate in such programs being twice as likely to be released. Additionally, participation in prison treatment programs significantly increased the likelihood of parole (OR= 3.583, $p < 0.001$), with applicants who participated in prison treatment being over 3.5 times more likely to be released than those who did not.

Looking closely at the significant predictors, the relevance of retributive factors can also be seen. Applicants who demonstrated a "change in understanding the seriousness of actions" (OR= 3.852, $p < 0.001$) were over 3.8 times more likely to be released than those who did not. Conversely, "harm to public trust in the CJS" significantly reduced the likelihood of parole (OR= 0.195, $p < 0.01$), with this category decreasing the odds of release by approximately 80.5%. "Length of sentence" also emerged as a significant predictor (OR= 0.959, p < 0.05), with each additional year reducing the odds of parole by approximately 4.1%. Furthermore, "criminal record" was a significant predictor (OR= 0.406, $p < 0.05$), with applicants who had a criminal record being 59.4% less likely to be granted parole. The insignificance of ethnicity in the models, which contrasts with previous findings (Huebner & Bynum, 2006), may be explained by the sample's demographic composition. The majority of the sample was Jewish, and Jewish prisoners made up a substantial portion (69%) of manslaughter cases. Furthermore, as mentioned, most committee chairpersons in Israel are Jewish (Gov, 2025), likely contributing to ethnicity's lack of significance in the analysis. This finding aligns with the sample and is consistent with some research in Israel (Danziger et al., 2011; Walk & Dagan, 2024), though not all (Avnaim & Guetzkow, in press).

4.1 Quantitative Insights

The quantitative findings indicate that despite operating under traditional risk and rehabilitation-oriented parole law, morality is part of the parole agenda. In fact, the board balances three competing forces – rehabilitation, risk, and morality – in its decision-making. As Model D demonstrates, retributive factors *make an incremental contribution to the cumulative variability accounted for in the board's decisions, beyond the utilitarian (risk and rehabilitation) factors*. This finding supports the notion that parole decision-making serves as a platform for managing conflicting penological, institutional, organizational, and political conceptions and influences (Lin et al., 2010; Paparozzi & Caplan, 2009).

As expected, the board views risk as crucial: a medium-high risk assessment reduced release prospects by 68.7%, consistent with previous literature (Caplan, 2007; Rhine et al., 2017). Prison treatment emerged as a robust and highly prevalent predictor of parole, as has been observed in several studies (Ouaknine et al., 2021; Rosenfeld & Noah, 2021; Vîlcică, 2018), supporting the notion that the board does not lose sight of rehabilitation (Walk & Dagan, 2024). Participation in prison treatment programs increased parole prospects by about 3.5 times over those who did not participate, and applicants with post-release rehabilitation programs were approximately twice as likely to be released. This emphasis on prison treatment in Israel may be explained by a 2012 reform that legislated a right to rehabilitation and education, which has been identified as a key factor for short-term prisoners (Ouaknine et al., 2021). With regard to retributive factors, specifically punishment-related factors, "severe medical condition" demonstrated no statistically significant relationship with the board's decision, likely due to its low prevalence and inconsistent application, possibly as this factor could be taken into consideration for medical parole in a separate track for dying prisoners (s.7). Second, the category of "insufficient time served" has shown conflicting results across studies (Caplan, 2007; Rieger & Serin, 2024) and may potentially overlap with "especially severe crime."

Crime-related factors also had a significant impact. For the released applicants, murderers served a longer (though not significantly longer) percentage of their sentence than did those convicted of manslaughter (77.4% versus 74.6%) and had substantially and significantly lower release rates (26.2% versus 39.8%). Among the crime-related factors, "especially severe crime" emerged as the most prevalent category (20.5%) with a significant association with parole decision, a finding consistent with previous research (Caplan & Kinnevy, 2010; Morgan & Smith, 2005; Rhine et al., 2017; Vîlcică, 2018).

The limited consideration given to "harm to public trust in the CJS" (6.2% prevalence), which showed a weak and insignificant association, can be explained by its narrow legal application reserved for "exceptional circumstances" (s.10(a); Dagan, 2023). Additionally, for each additional year of sentence length, the odds of parole release decreased by approximately 4.1%. This finding aligns with the board's more retributive orientation in serious cases, as observed in several studies (Caplan, 2007; Caplan & Kinnevy, 2010; Morgan & Smith, 2005; Vîlcică, 2018; Young et al., 2016).

Regarding *moral character-related factors*, the findings indicated that "admits crime" (43.4% prevalence) and "expresses remorse" (42.5% prevalence) were substantially prevalent and significantly associated with parole decisions, highlighting the board's focus on "internal" morality rather than merely "external" participation in rehabilitation (Vîlcică, 2018). Furthermore, applicants who demonstrated a "change in insight" were almost four times more likely to be released than those who did not. This finding confirms the importance of "insight" for long-term parole decisions (Dalke, 2023; Young et al., 2016). Possibly, the board's emphasis on "insight" may represent a more acceptable way to consider the legally exceptional factor of "especially severe crime" (s.10(a)), similar to the increased prevalence of "insight" found in the U.S. context after the rejection of parole decisions based explicitly on crime severity was invalidated by courts (Dalke, 2023). Additionally, "criminal record," associated with greater immoral character and culpability by scholars (Roberts, 2008), was found to be a significant predictor of parole denial, consistent with previous studies (Caplan, 2007; Houser et al., 2019).

The quantitative analysis is not without limitations. First, as the data were collected from the start of the PRA archives in 2018, they may underrepresent the full population of parole applicants. Second, there is an unknown number of applicants who "max out" and do not apply for parole (Rosenfeld & Noah, 2021). As we do not have access to this data (sourced from the PRA), future studies could address this gap. Third, the focus on homicide cases potentially skews the results and limits their applicability to moral labor in other parole contexts (e.g., sex-crime cases). Fourth, numbers may not reveal the full story (Weinshall, 2024). For example, it's possible that at least some retributive parole factors/categories (e.g., "*crime severity*") are not genuinely retributive, as the board may consider them primarily for assessing risk rather than retribution. Finally, another limitation concerns the potential for post-hoc rationalization in parole board decisions. The board's written factors might not represent genuine independent considerations but rather post-hoc justification construction (Dalke & McConnell, 2024).

Thus, to deepen the analysis, a qualitative approach is required. The qualitative analysis, complements the quantitative findings by shedding light on the nuanced discourses underlying parole hearings, offering depth beyond numerical data. These qualitative findings illuminate the complex narratives of crime seriousness, punishment severity, and moral character, either independently or together with the risk and rehabilitation discourses. This rich narrative context provides a comprehensive understanding of parole as not merely a bureaucratic risk-assessment process but as a moral forum reflecting evolving moral sentiments over time, aimed at "doing late justice."

5 The Moral Theatre of Parole: Qualitative Findings

The following presents the moral "theatre" of parole (Goffman, 1959/1980) based on a qualitative analysis of the parole hearings' transcripts in chronological order of the parole actors' arguments: AGRs, SVs, applicants, and finally the board's decisions. The moral labor of parole actors during the hearings stands side by side with traditional narratives of risk and rehabilitation, which were found to a larger or smaller extent in all cases analyzed, as expected in the utilitarian risk-oriented sphere of parole. Figure 1 summarizes the qualitative analysis.

5.1 "Dr. Jekyll and Mr. Hyde": The Moral Labor of the Attorney General

With rare exceptions, the AGRs opened the hearings. The AGRs' overall position was resistant to release (85.1% overall resistance rate), consistent with the overall resistant prosecutors approach in previous studies (Dagan, 2023; Murcia, 2022; Rosenfeld & Noah, 2021). The AGRs were risk-focused and punitive: "We see before us first of all the crime severity and the prisoner's risk" (case-31357-07-21). Beyond pointing to applicants' future risk and poor rehabilitation prospects – common in their arguments – the AGRs' moral labor included two key themes: *judicializing the parole hearings* and *managing a moral-risk matrix*.

5.1.1 Judicializing Hearings: Extending the Sentencing Voice into Parole

A central theme in AGRs' moral labor was the judicialization of the parole hearing process. However, this judicialization did not center on preserving procedural integrity or safeguarding the board's independence from undue political influence. Instead, the AGRs judicialized the hearings by employing three narratives that mimicked and prolonged the role of the sentencing judge.

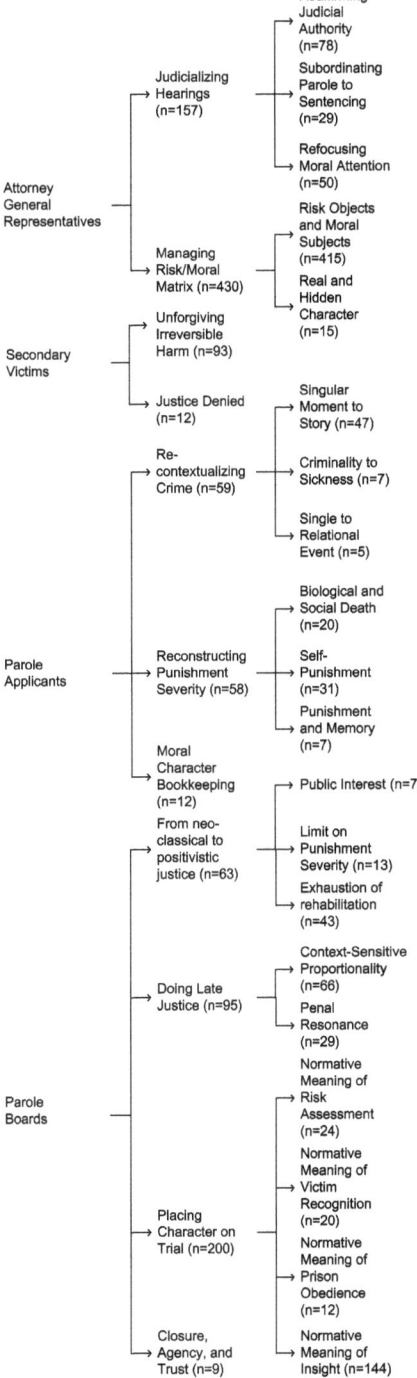

Figure 1 The moral meaning of parole: Qualitative findings

Reaffirming Judicial Authority

The AGRs' arguments were based on the written materials in the parole dossier; the AGRs did not call witnesses and resisted applicants' attempts to call them. The arguments presented by AGRs typically began with a quotation or paraphrase of the key normative and factual determinations made at trial and sentencing. With very few exceptions, the AGRs devoted a substantial portion of their argument – often, more than half – to repeating the court's narrative and comparing it to the applicants' story of the crime in minute detail, as found among U.S. parole decision-makers (Young & Chimowitz, 2022). Seventy-eight AGRs meticulously policed even the slightest deviation in the applicants' account from the judicially established narrative, including discrepancies such as the specific weapon used, the exact location of the body, or the number of wounds inflicted. The AGRs juxtaposed the official legal "story" of the crime as expressed in the verdict and sentencing remarks, and the applicants' "story" of the crime as expressed in the police interrogation, trial testimony, sentencing hearing, in front of correctional officers or during the parole hearing. One may wonder about the significance of reciting at length the judicial narrative that took place decades before the hearing as part of an allegedly future-looking parole hearing. The board itself wondered the same. Nonetheless, the AGRs consistently insisted on this repetition, justifying this practice by emphasizing its importance in highlighting the discrepancies between the official narrative and the applicants' version of events:

> The board asks me not to repeat every detail and every account of the court's holding ... The board is right. We are not in a sentencing appeal, but this is important to us, that the prisoner's narrative is different [from the official account]. This fact-related gap is important and relevant. (case-1920-02-18)

The AGRs required the applicants to fully internalize and identify with the judicial, official story of the crime and sternly criticized applicants who were viewed as failing to do so. Such applicants were perceived as failing to show "insight" into their crime (sec. 5.4.3), and their rehabilitation was deemed superficial:

> The prisoner gave a completely different story from the judicial determination to the [prison] social worker, portraying himself in a much more positive light, standing up to protect others .... and he [just] found himself in a situation ... however, in the sentencing remarks it is explicitly written that he took a knife and went to look for the [victim]. This has implications for the prisoner's crime internalization and casts doubt on his commitment to the treatment. (case-74933-10-18)

As part of endorsing the judicial narrative, the AGRs expected applicants to acknowledge their crime as a *public-legal wrong* rather than merely a private conflict between two individuals: "I expect that when the prisoner comes before the board, he will stand up honestly and say: 'I killed a human being, I understand that I committed ... *the most serious violent crime in the criminal code*'" (case-40977-03-19).[25] In such cases, the AGRs essentially acted "as if" the sentencing judge were there at the hearing, becoming an absent-present actor at the hearings.

The rehearsal of the judicial narrative of the crime, and the requirement that applicants reaffirm this narrative, enabled the AGRs to advance three aims. First, they could frame the applicants as "juridical" rather than purely "clinical" subjects (Bourdieu, 1987; Foucault, 1977). As such, the moral lens of guilt and desert, the locus of homicide sentencing, becomes as significant to their assessment as their therapeutic needs or risk. Second, the applicants' reaffirmation of the judicial narrative in their own words reinforces the judicial authority as symbolically present in the hearing in a process that could, in and of itself, be viewed as undermining the court's authority to impose a life sentence (or significant prison term). Finally, in internalizing the judicial story, the applicants exclude any alternative explanation for their crime, reaffirm their lack of moral standing to demand their release, and display their remorse during the hearing as morally expected.

Subordinating Parole to Sentencing

Along with reaffirming the judicial authority, in cases of especially serious homicide (e.g., multiple victims, murder of a child), the AGRs subordinated the board's decision-making to the court's judgments regarding the applicants' crime and character. This narrative positioned the judicial process as a moral frame, and a source of pressure on the board, to "re-censure" the applicants (Aviram, 2020; Dagan, 2023):

> Not every day do we see that a court ... [expresses] such disgust in the sentencing remarks, and this disgust must be considered by the board today. *This judicial verdict and its meaning are a binding determination [for the board]*. (case-22222-04-14)

This narrative aimed to ensure that the board adhered to past judicial censuring determinations without deviating by releasing the applicants:

> *The court's verdict is the starting point for the hearing* ... this case shook the foundations of society, an act of exceptional severity. The act's trauma went beyond the immediate family circle and spread to the general public and the media. (case-13842-08-14)

---

[25] Emphases in the quotes are the author's.

In this narrative, 29 AGRs sought to amalgamate sentencing and parole messages and the general punitive voices of the unforgiving SVs (sec. 5.2.1), public opinion, and/or the media, which served as a "moral memory bloc" to bind the board to the court's censure (Aviram, 2020). In this way, as much as unjustified parole release undermines sentencing justice, a justified parole denial reaffirms the court's moral authority:

> The board perceives itself as a rehabilitative body, but it has another role as well ... the purpose of punishment is also to realize the public interest. *It is not appropriate that what the judicial system sought to realize at sentencing is then undermined by the board* ... The board must ask if we want to live in a society where a prisoner convicted of such a serious crime should be paroled ... the board doesn't operate in a vacuum but functions as an integral part of the justice system, representing the values and principles that underpin our society .... and acts, broadly, as the public guardian. (case-35845-12-16)

As this narrative suggests, the AGRs established an "intertextuality" (Eco, 1985) between sentencing and parole moral labor, emphasizing that both should serve to promote broader societal "values" and the "public interest," objectives that extend beyond rehabilitation and risk. The reframing of the board as not merely a "rehabilitative board" means that the criteria of "justice" and "values" are also applied to parole decision-making. Furthermore, as connected to the public meaning of sentencing, some AGRs even encouraged the board in severe cases to open its closed doors, to achieve a moral and public impact similar to that of a sentencing hearing. As one AGR articulated, "punitive considerations should apply to parole, it concerns the public interest, and the public has the right to know" (case-35845-12-16). In rendering parole decisions public, the AGRs reframed the board as a second court, public and punitive, beyond the real sentencing courtroom.

Refocusing Moral Attention

Finally, the AGRs harnessed the court's determinations to redirect the board's moral attention toward the severity of the crime and the victims' suffering, rather than the applicants' pains, rehabilitation efforts, or post-release plans. Fifty AGRs encouraged the board to save their empathy for the SVs rather than for applicants, suggesting a "zero-sum game": "When considering the difficulty of the prisoner and his family, please remember that [the victim], a boy loved by his family and friends, had his life cut short by a stab which pierced his heart" (case-31357-07-21). They also established through the court's judgments a "moral boundary" between the victim's image as kind, moral, and innocent, and the applicant's immorality and inhumanity (Herbert, 2024): "The court defined the murder as a cynical, despicable, and inhuman act toward his good friend ... someone who was like a saving angel for the prisoner, a good and supportive figure whom he could rely on" (case-56855-12-20).

In re-focusing the board's moral focus, the AGRs also sought to shift the emphasis of the hearing from the applicants' rehabilitation to the public meaning of their crime as expressed through sentencing:

> Even a rehabilitation post-release program cannot justify parole and does not ease the serious harm to the public, to the judicial and law enforcement system, or to general deterrence if he were to be released ... no individual, group, or religious therapy, even provided by the IPS, can restore to the families their loved ones or relieve their trauma, pain, and loss they experienced due to the prisoner's crimes. (case-27835-03-15)

Seeking to shift the attention away from the applicants, AGRs frequently criticized applicants for overemphasizing their suffering or losses rather than focusing on their victims: "He focuses on the private price he pays ... and the harm suffered from not being able to have a family" (case-17636-05-16). These AGRs thus demarcated a boundary between the SVs' suffering, which deserved recognition as morally legitimate, and the applicants' suffering, which became largely irrelevant to the parole decision-making and did not deserve to be recognized.

In sum, the AGRs harnessed and expanded the legitimacy and symbolic capital of the "juridical field" of parole (Bourdieu, 1987), allowing them to legitimize the board as an extension of the court's moral communication. Further, the use of judicial rhetoric allowed the AGRs to be viewed as merely citing past judicial reasoning, subtly "bypassing" possible criticism for transforming parole hearings into punitive re-censuring forums.

5.1.2 Managing the Risk/Moral Matrix

Between Risk Objects and Moral Subjects

Alongside judicializing parole, the AGRs focused, in largely every case, on analyzing the correctional data in the parole dossier, including clinical reports, psychological risk assessments, or records from prison officers. Unlike the *crime*-oriented work of sentencing, here the AGRs conducted a deeper examination of applicants' *character*. The AGRs constructed a hybrid risk/character assessment that adopted the strictest interpretations of neoclassical and positivistic theories. Often, doing so included presenting the applicants' immorality on the basis of their crime and their depraved character:

> The prisoner's acts ... *degrade the value of human life's sanctity.* [The prisoner] intentionally led to the deaths of two girls *without mercy* for the victims' families. The court observed: 'These acts require a strict punishment at a high level.' The court also noted that the [the prisoner] did not prevent the murders, took an active part in committing them, *did not regret the acts* after the murders [and] did not report them to the police. (case-21397-09-17)

However, as the argument progressed, the AGR shifted to framing the applicant as "dangerous" and "out of control," "anti-social," "schizophrenic," and having "abnormal thinking":

> The psychiatric assessment indicates the presence of abnormal thinking and possible schizophrenia, difficulties in judgment, sinking into primitive fantasies ... feelings of unreality, faulty thoughts and confusion, and it is clear that there is significant risk ... all the factors that cause her disinhibition are still present today ... the risk she poses is evident from the psychiatric diagnosis ... a lack of insight and anti-social behavior. (case-21397-09-17)

By oscillating between neoclassical and positivistic discourses, the AGRs effectively framed the applicants as the "worst of the worst" of both worlds, being both "risk objects" and "moral subjects" (Hannah-Moffat, 1999). On the one hand, they were depicted as being able to distinguish right from wrong and thus were deemed deserving of strict retribution for failing to conduct themselves morally. On the other hand, they were portrayed as pathological "others," subject to deterministic psycho-socio-biological forces and thus should be imprisoned as long as possible for public safety (Garland, 2001). The categories of risk/character for the AGRs were thus fluid, shifting between different, possibly conflicting, discourses, that could reinforce each other.

Between Real and Hidden Character

The risk/moral matrix was further used by the AGRs to question the very epistemological possibility of fully "knowing" the applicants' character. The AGRs implied, both directly and indirectly, that the applicants were merely presenting an idealized-performative version of themselves, offering a compelling "front" as truly reformed desisters, tailored to impress their parole audience (Goffman, 1959/1980). According to this perspective, fifteen applicants were projecting a moral "false" public self while concealing a "real" self that was immoral and dangerous. Applicants were often framed as giving a misleading performance, as one AGR argued: "*He is Dr. Jekyll and Mr. Hyde.* He tells the board what the board wants to hear ... We need what he does, not what he says to the board" (case-35845-12-16). Thus, to expose this hidden immorality and risk, the AGRs emphasized the necessity of cultivating suspicion, allowing them to know applicants' "hidden layer":

> The applicant] has indeed undergone some process in prison, but ... every person, and certainly prisoner, has a visible layer – what he projects to the world and what he wants others to think and see about him, and he also has a hidden layer – things beneath the surface that he prefers people not know. (case-52545-08-21)

To "cultivate suspicion," the AGRs used the judicial or correctional assessments, sometimes determined decades ago, regarding the applicants' "true" character, as one AGR argued (even using the word "defendant" in his statement):

> The court elaborated extensively on the cruelty and despicableness of the defendant's acts ... noting that he [showed] exceptional ability to pretend throughout police investigations ... The court was impressed that he was a "manipulator, self-serving, accustomed to living for years in lies" ... The court then reviewed the defendant's false versions, defined them as fantastical, and rejected his case out of hand. (case-56855-12-20)

Such portrayals of the applicants conveyed AGRs' sense of mistrust regarding the authenticity of their character transformation: "I believe there is always a need for skepticism. Anybody that makes decisions must exercise extreme caution ... the impression is of a prisoner who is manipulative, cold-blooded, and sophisticated" (case-77504-12-20).

Deeply suspicious of applicants' perceived "double self" (Goffman, 1959/1980), AGRs demanded a perfect and constant moral character performance, which should be "high and stable" (case-52425-07-17) and "flawless" (case-59589-01-18). As one AGR argued: "The process must be perfect and whole. Whole about the way [in which it is carried out], and perfect concerning the substantive achievements" (case-15008-07-20). By requiring perfection, the AGRs effectively demanded no less than "risk elimination" (case-77504-12-20), imposing a "very heavy burden" on the applicants (case-41810-12-18).

The narrative of character perfection and overall performance, however, was challenged by the applicants and their counsel as being unrealistic for long-term prisoners. One board decision called for more realistic expectations:

> A prisoner leaving prison is a person whose past will always cast a shadow over their future. A prisoner will never be a perfect person, as they carry a very problematic and negative burden on their shoulders ... However, the board must examine whether the prisoner is worthy of release despite his flaws. (case-38711-03-17)

In sum, the AGRs essentially extended the past-looking, punitive, and adversarial sentencing to the parole hearings, to reinforce the immorality of the applicants' *crime*. The immoral character that emerged from the applicants' crimes even "bled" into decision-making that was meant to be based on their changed character. Later, both clinical and risk discourses were harnessed to construct the applicants' *character* as both immoral and dangerous, and thus fixated and unchanged.

5.2 "You destroyed a family": The Moral Labor of Secondary Victims

Following the AGRs' arguments, the SVs typically voiced their arguments. The contributions of the SVs – usually the deceased's parents or children – were highly emotional, involving crying, shouting, and halting speech. The SVs submitted an overall 100 written VISs, and 21 SVs also expressed verbal VISs. The SVs showed 93% resistance to release, consistent with previous studies (Caplan, 2012; Roberts, 2008).[26] Their narratives focused on (a) *unforgiving the irreversible individual harm done to them*, and (b) *resistance to the perceived injustice of parole*.

5.2.1 Unforgiving the Irreversible Individual Harm

The SVs' focus was on censuring applicants in stark terms, describing them as a "ticking bomb" (case-26098-03-15), "despicable" (case-13842-08-14), "worthless" (case-47246-06-20), or similar terms. The AGRs, as noted, often framed the crime as a *public-legal* wrong (sec. 5.1.1). In contrast, the SVs sought to personalize the crime and reclaim the "conflict" as their own (Christie, 1977). They personified their dead loved ones as living individuals rather than faceless objects or abstract interests. For example, one SV pleaded: "I ask you to put my child's memory before your eyes, a happy, loving, funny child (crying)" (case-30504-05-19). To achieve this individualization of harm, some SVs reproached the applicants via a form of "moral education" (Hampton, 1984):

> You [the applicant] knew [the victim's name]. Why did you kill him? For a trivial matter. The only one who has the right to take a person's life is God. He decides, not humans ... You should have thought about it carefully ... Why didn't you think about this before the murder? ... You should have drunk some cold water and moved on. But look at what you've done to yourself as well. It's such a pity. (case-30504-05-19)

Similar to the AGRs' narratives, the SVs re-enacted the crime's details (sec. 5.1.1.), presenting the visceral reality and the suffering imposed on their deceased

---

[26] Agreement with parole among SVs occurred in cases of *Sulha* (Arabic: traditional reconciliation), or in cases of relatives of women who killed their abusive husbands.

love one and themselves. The SVs provided vivid and often graphic descriptions, such as the burning of the victim's body or the exact shape and location of wounds. They then moved on to expressing their suffering, including eulogy-like narratives characterized by mourning for the lives that they (and their loved ones) *could have lived*. These narratives revived the "moral memory" (Aviram, 2020) of their deceased family members, effectively transforming the hearing into a memorial ceremony, pointing to "linking objects" (Riches & Dawson, 1998) such as favorite music or clothing to evoke the victim's memory:

> We are 10 orphans. Our father was an exemplary man, who helped and supported us. He was a listening ear, he was everything to us . . . He did not get to see my children or grandson . . . For 22 years I've had my father's handkerchief with me. I haven't washed the handkerchief, and I just sniff it . . . Every Friday I go to the cemetery to visit him . . . It's so hard for us. (case-44972-09-17)

The SVs described at length how the harm caused by the crime continued to unfold long after sentencing time, consistent with other contexts of grieving homicide (Riches & Dawson, 1998) (King, 2004). The SVs portrayed the crime as a sudden, violent, and unnatural event that created a profound rupture in their worldview:

> [This] harsh day that shook our world changed our lives irreversibly . . . the murderer killed a family for all generations ahead . . . we are asking the board to consider the harmed side, me, my children, grandchildren, and this [harm] will pass to future generations . . . the prisoner punished us for our whole lives. (case-19975-07-22)

The SVs emphasized the grave and irreparable nature of the harm caused by the crime: "Our beloved [deceased's name] is under a stone; she will remain forever 19-years-old, *nothing will bring her back to life*" (case-26098-03-15). For the SVs, no moral, emotional, or material reparation can be achieved between them and the applicants. They conveyed a sense of eternal unforgiveness, firmly rejecting the possibility of moral restoration through punishment. One father said the following:

> I want to tell you [the applicant] that until my last day, I will not forgive you, neither you nor your friends . . . I would not have wished such a thing even on my enemies. You have ruined my life. I have become a sick man. We all have become needy people . . . Why do I deserve this? (crying). You have finished the life of my entire family . . . I am not forgiving you or your friends . . . Nothing that you say will help. (case-30504-05-19)

The following dialogue between an applicant and an SV demonstrates this unforgiving dynamic:

> The applicant: I am ashamed of what I did, I am willing to sit for another 10 years so that you, the family, will forgive me . . . I have been living in hell for

21 years. I am ashamed of what I did, I am a terrible person ... I seek forgiveness (crying) ...

The victim's brother: [You] didn't just murder my brother; over the past 21 years, four of my sisters died, one after another. I was on medication, I had a catheterization, diabetes ... My brother was righteous; if you had been at his funeral, you would have heard the eulogies ... he helped anyone in need, and gave to everyone with an open heart, he had such a pure heart. How could you kill such a man? (case-56048-09-16)

Such SVs described their inability to reconcile the moral injustice of a kind, generous, and loving individual meeting such a fate – one marked by brutal and unexplained evil – as found in previous victims' contexts (Hadar & Gal, 2023).

Some SVs combined the personalization of their loss with a broader appeal to societal interests. By harnessing their tragedy to a larger context, these SVs sought to influence the board's decision to deny parole: "Many eyes are facing you ... we are witnessing murder after murder against women [in our society]; the deterrence and punishment are not severe enough apparently" (case-26098-03-15). Such SVs urged the board to send a public message that crime does not pay, that crime severity remains static, and that censure and deterrence should counterbalance the applicants' rehabilitation:

The time does not mitigate the magnitude of the crime ... Rejecting parole is in the public interest and counterweighs his rehabilitation ... considering the dramatic rise in murders, the board must deliver a clear message to every murderer, wherever he is, that no good prison conduct or rehabilitation will atone for his crime ... the struggle is for all those victims who are not here to raise their voices. (case-54100-03-19)

These SVs thus emphasized that punishment should endure over time so that the irreparable harm done to them could, at least, benefit the larger public, being a moral lesson for the future.

5.2.2 Justice Denied: Ensuring the Justice of Parole

The SVs also saw the hearing as an opportunity to question both the original sentence and the possibility of parole for homicide cases. They expressed feelings of being marginalized throughout the criminal process, with the parole stage representing the final manifestation of such injustices. They conveyed frustration at being perceived as "outsiders" within the professionalized-legalized parole hearings (Bibas, 2012; Roberts & Erez, 2004): "We have been cut off from the entire legal process for 22 years" (case-47246-06-20) or "This is the first time that I am speaking with [the applicant]" (case-30504-05-19).

Specifically, in cases of murder, the SVs expressed confusion and frustration regarding the true meaning of a mandatory life sentence in line with the argument that a life sentence, as an open-ended punishment, is a "sentence nobody can understand" (Mitchell & Roberts, 2012, p. 36). None of the SVs believed that the punishment served at the time of the hearing was commensurate with the severity of the applicants' crime. The SVs viewed the very possibility of a sentence that was not a literal "eye for an eye" as leniency and, thus, any further mitigation as unjust: "I don't think he should be given a reward; his mere being alive is more than enough [crying]" (case-25827-08-14) or "It looks to me illogical [to release him]. Why? Would my husband come back?" (case-56855-12-18).

In expressing such views, these SVs emphasized the injustice of parole by juxtaposing the applicant and the deceased victim, highlighting the imperfect justice that arises when the applicant's continued living is contrasted with a loved one's death (Aviram, 2020). These SVs articulated an existential sense of "moral injury" (Dagan & Rennie, 2025), describing the emotional toll of seeing the applicants alive – and even rehabilitated – while their own lives remained irreparably shattered. They asked the board to shift the focus of "rehabilitation" from the applicants to the SVs themselves: "I have suffered so much; at age 13 my childhood was over ... the murderer was rehabilitated, but what about us?" (case-56855-12-20). Accordingly, these SVs argued that a "whole life" sentence represented the *minimum standard of justice* and, thus, parole constituted a profoundly unjust outcome:

> *The sister of the deceased*: From the start, we could not understand [why] the punishment imposed on my brother's murderer was so mild ...
>
> *The board*: The board draws the [secondary] victim's attention to the fact that the prisoner was sentenced to two life sentences. The President then commuted the sentence to 35 years. The board has clarified to the [secondary] victim the legal processes that have taken place until now.
>
> *The sister*: I was not aware of all previous procedures. The board's explanation made me feel even more frustrated with the system ... This mild sentence is unclear to us. At least ensure that this sentence will be served fully ... a life sentence is imposed on a murderer because there is no way to pay such a debt to society ... this murderer has no place but to remain behind bars for as long as possible. (case-13842-08-14)

In manslaughter cases, the SVs perceived parole as a double injustice, rendering the sentence a "surreal" outcome, given the applicants' reduced punishment due to plea-based mitigation:

> *The mother of the deceased*: The possibility to release [him] is completely surreal for us ... he already got his reward by a plea bargain ... we are

begging that the murderer not be given leniency. The murderer must serve his entire punishment until the last day ... this is inconceivable, to release him in just a few days. (case-30504-05-19)

The SVs criticized the legal definition of the crime, expressing outrage over how the applicants were convicted of "manslaughter" for an act they perceived as *intentional* premeditated killing:

> *The son of the deceased*: To say that there was no premeditation is problematic. He went to get a weapon and returned [to the scene] ... he was charged with manslaughter. If he had been charged with murder, he wouldn't have received only 12 years, which is a joke ... If he is released, it would be a travesty of justice. (case-60665-03-19)

In cases of murder, SVs sought to morally distinguish between different kinds of murder by advocating for parole denial. As one SV stated: "Even for murder there are different levels. This is the highest level [of crime], a cold-blooded premeditated murder" (case-13842-08-14). In doing so, the SVs challenged not only parole but extended their moral outrage to criticize the original sentence.

In response to these perceived injustices, the SVs urged the board to deny parole, with some even referring to the board as a court: "I count on the court to do justice and keep him where he is" (case-56855-12-18). Parole release, in contrast, was viewed as an act of cruelty toward the SVs and an extension of the harm caused by the crime: "Our lives depend on your decision ... Anyone who shows mercy to the cruel will end up being cruel to the merciful" (case-54100-03-19). Rather than granting parole, the SVs called on the board to delay the "legal closure" of the crime story and preserve the victim's memory (Meyers, 2016): "At least honor my brother a little bit and let this despicable murderer remain behind bars for as long as possible" (case-13842-08-14).

In sum, the SVs rarely offered *new risk*-related information to the hearings. Instead, unforgiving the irreversible harm done them and resisting the perceived injustice of parole, they request "doing late justice" via parole denial.

5.3 "You see in front of you a monster, but ...": The Moral Labor of Parole Applicants

The applicants and their counsel concluded the argument session of the hearings.[27] Similar to the AGRs' and SVs' narratives, the applicants' narratives went well

---

[27] The narratives of the applicants' counsel and of the applicants themselves considerably overlap and thus I will analyze mainly the applicants' narratives, referring to key distinctions between them when needed. A detailed comparison between the two remains for a future study.

beyond risk/rehabilitation considerations. Instead, a significant portion of their narratives focused on addressing the moral conundrum of parole: how to morally justify their release after having committed one of the most serious crimes possible. In other words, the applicants sought to manage their "parole deservingness" (Lavin-Loucks, 2002).

Mirroring the SVs' narratives regarding the irreversibility of the crime (sec. 5.2.1.), thirty-five applicants expressed existential despair over their inability to change the past: "If only I could turn the wheel back for one minute, I would give all I have for it" (case-65061-06-18). Consequently, such applicants often accepted their moral *un-deservingness* of parole: "Do I deserve anything? No ... my hands are stained with blood ... I will never be able to undo the harm I caused" (case-28745-08-14). For these applicants, the punishment they felt they deserved extended beyond incarceration to include deprivation of social relationships or even death: "I did the worst thing possible and deserve punishment ... If you let me judge myself, I would impose on myself a whole life in prison, I deserve to be without a mother (crying)" (case-31992-02-22). As such, the applicants' narratives focused on managing their guilt through (a) *re-contextualizing the moral meaning of crime*, (b) *reconstructing punishment severity*, and (c) *moral character bookkeeping*.

5.3.1 Recontextualizing the Moral Meaning of Crime

The applicants devoted much of their narratives to reconstructing the moral meaning of their crime. Popular cultural perceptions of "murder" often depict it as a shocking one-time encounter between an entirely innocent victim and a premeditating, evil, sadistic monster (Rock, 1998). In contrast, the legal definition of murder typically views it narrowly as the intentional, and sometimes spontaneous, act of causing another person's death, regardless of the underlying reasons/contexts (Ashworth & Horder, 2013). The applicants resisted both the cultural and legal framings of their actions. Instead, they invited the board to view their crimes in a context-sensitive way – namely, given sociodemographic factors, cultural patterns, offenders' and victims' personal characteristics, and contextual and situational factors (Dobash et al., 2004). The applicants (or their counsel) reminded the board: "There is factual truth and legal truth, and the *real truth* sometimes lies somewhere in between" (case-25827-08-14).

Openly denying the crime was rare, as such a stance would render parole prospects unrealistic. Only six applicants outright denied their crime: "Don't make me confess to something I didn't do" (case-21146-11-12).[28] Thirty-nine applicants fully accepted their label as "murderers" (e.g., "I know that I am despicable and a murderer" (case-13842-08-14)). The most prevalent narrative was to accept guilt but with qualifications, often employing the formula: "I am guilty, *but.*" To illustrate: "I express my deepest and sincerest remorse and take full responsibility, but at the time of the crime, I was ill-equipped to understand the gravity of my actions" (case-32840-02-19). To reconstruct the morality of their crime, these applicants pointed to the criminological and moral forces that motivated their actions and emotions, even when not recognized by murder law. They expressed that they held at least some moral standing to ask for their release, given that the real immorality of their crime, when considering the broader picture of their act, was quite different from the law's narrow and flat view. They recontextualized their crimes in three main ways.

(a) *From a singular moment to a story.* Forty-seven applicants began their arguments by narrating their biographies through a broad criminological lens that alluded to weak self-control, negative associations with older offenders, or strains that stood at the ground of their crimes (Agnew, 1992; Gottfredson & Hirschi, 1990). They framed the crime not as a singular moment but as the culmination of a long downward trajectory, moving from a snapshot to a panoramic view of their crime. These narratives frequently included "sad stories" (Maruna, 2001) of childhood experiences marked by neglect, abuse, and poverty, which they argued naturally led them to "drift" to a life of crime (Matza, 1964): "I grew up with a distorted view of the world . . . surrounded by violence, with an abusive and drug-addicted father . . . I believed that violence was the only way to navigate my world" (case-55097-05-19) or "I was a boy from the hood, I carried out crimes to eat, not to get rich" (case-54326-01-19). Through these accounts, the applicants acknowledged that they *harmed* others, but tried to mitigate their moral responsibility for committing serious *moral wrongs* (Jarman, 2020; Sykes & Matza, 1957). Several applicants also described how they were "tricked" into a life of crime by the influence and pressure of older criminals:

> I grew up in a poor neighborhood, surrounded by criminals . . . I became deeply involved with them. They asked me to be a partner in crime. I hesitated. They said, "We're taking guns, stealing cars." . . . I said I wanted to try. There were revolvers, gloves, and a stolen car, so I was afraid. I told them I regretted it, I didn't want to, I was extremely scared. One of them told

---

[28] In some U.S. jurisdictions and England and Wales, parole denial based on an innocence claim is unlawful (PSO, 2011, s.4.14.5). Several other U.S. states allow parole rejection based on denial of guilt (Medwed, 2008). In Israel, denial can be used against the applicant, but this does not categorically exclude parole (*Ganame v. Parole Board*, 2016).

> me I couldn't regret it now ... He pressured me so much. He said, If you're not with us, you're against us ... I did it out of fear. (case-4706-02-19)

Other applicants described how they embraced the "code of the street" (Anderson, 1999), adopting sub-culture values of aggressiveness and disrespect for authority through socialization with peers or significant others:

> My acts stemmed from the criminal environment in which I grew up ... I don't condone my actions and don't justify them, but I had a misguided belief that I could resolve issues through the code of the street, without involving law enforcement or seeking help from state services. I used violence and threats, which shaped my upbringing. (case-12104-06-18)

Several applicants presented a narrative of an "out-of-character" act conducted by an "ordinary man" in an extreme moment of passion, or a "mistake" rather than a premeditated act (Dobash et al., 2004): "I harmed by mistake, I had no intention to kill him, my decision was wrong" (case-25722-09-20) or "I didn't know how to behave under stress and I lost control and committed the crime" (case-53385-01-20). Framing their crime as a one-time mistake, often made in a specific moment of pressure, these applicants expressed disbelief at having committed such a severe crime (Crewe et al., 2020), describing it as fundamentally at odds with their core moral self: "It is hard for me to believe that I did it; it is so distant from me" (case-25827-08-14).

(b) *From criminality to sickness.* Seven applicants adopted a positivistic form of "denial of responsibility" (Sykes & Matza, 1957). Drawing on the language of Twelve-Step programs, these applicants framed their crimes as motivated by the "addiction disease," arguing that their actions should be viewed as symptoms of illness rather than reflections of an evil core character: "I want to express my deepest remorse for my acts ... I was not thinking about the victim or the consequences of my acts ... I was addicted, at the bottom of the barrel" (case-20006-06-16). These applicants linked their crimes to impaired mental health, suggesting diminished culpability: "[My crime] was a one-time event triggered by a psychotic episode ... I begged for medication ... but the psychiatrist disagreed" (case-28683-11-19). They contextualized their crime beyond both the narrow legal definition of "murder" and their popular cultural image as "monsters":

> You see in front of you a monster, but [I] was a young girl [at the time of the crime], with a mentally ill mother, living on the streets with an older man who beat [me], and then I committed [my] crimes. (case-21397-09-17)

They thus distanced themselves from the traditional view of murderers as cold-blooded rational actors, presenting themselves more as people in need, struggling with the strains of street life.

(c) *From a single to a relational event.* Five applicants contextualized their guilt by framing their crime as a result of a complex "duet" between themselves and their victims (May, 1999; Rock, 1998). This narrative, however, was rare and was typically articulated by applicants' counsel rather than by applicants themselves. Possibly, this rarity stemmed from the narrative's tendency to reverse the offender-victim symmetry, blaming the victim, and contradicting the official account of the crime:

> [The victim] was a piece of work ... He threatened the [applicant's] parents. [The applicant] didn't just go and carry out a murder just like that, as part of the world of crime. [The applicant] acted to preempt what they were going to do to him. He was threatened by a major criminal. (case-12104-06-18)

Another example of such contextualization was when a killing was framed as a response to an abusive partner – the only way to escape the misery of domestic violence (four applicants):

> I married the deceased [victim] who terrorized me ... my whole body had scars, you can't imagine the terror I lived in ... He was a gambler, came back at night, suddenly he'd throw [things] at the child ... I wanted to protect my children. I had nowhere to go, no one heard me. So I decided to take the law into my own hands ... you can't imagine what kind of man I lived with ... There was such immense pain; I couldn't control it. (case-24713-05-17)

In contextualizing their guilt and "de-idealizing" the victim (Christie, 1986), these applicants sought to humanize their actions as less morally reprehensible, and even, as morally even if not legally justifiable. They were essentially moral and far from the ideal type of "cold-blooded murderer" or "monster."

5.3.2 Reconstructing Punishment Severity

Aside from reconstructing the severity of their crime, applicants reframed the severity of their punishment through the hearing. Through this narrative, they sought to challenge the morality of their continued punishment as it did not accord with the moral wrongness of their crime.

Embodying Biological and Social Death

Applicants detailed the destructive realities of life imprisonment and its profound impact, aligning their experiences with the key pains of long-term imprisonment described in the literature (Crewe et al., 2020; Hulley et al., 2016; Kazemian & Travis, 2015). Lifers, in particular, emphasized the unique suffering associated with ageing or illness. They vividly described the physical deterioration caused by illness, which they perceived as a dehumanizing experience, and portrayed themselves as having transitioned from "criminals" to barely functioning "patients" due to severe conditions such as diabetes, respiratory diseases, or cancer:

> My daily routine in prison is affected by my health condition ... in the morning I go to the clinic for my insulin injection. I return to my cell and wait for ... another insulin injection ... I'm not the same person I used to be. I used to be able to do everything myself, but now I struggle with even the simplest tasks. I have back problems and it's hard for me to move. My pain is constant ... Sometimes I cry until morning. (case-62363-12-18)

The applicants' biological deterioration had implications for the justice and humanity of their continued imprisonment, as one applicant's counsel argued:

> There is a level of desert that society should consider, even in a case of manslaughter, for a person who has been in prison since the age of 20. Today he is 35-years-old, his healthy, vital, and good years were spent behind bars ... but the life expectancy for a dialysis patient is shortened by 30 years ... this means that he has about 14 years left. (case-55097-05-19)

Applicants' narratives of physical powerlessness, particularly those of elderly and chronically ill applicants, exemplify the destructive impact of life imprisonment on their present and future lives. The release of such applicants is therefore portrayed as less morally problematic, and in some cases, even morally deserved. Six applicants framed themselves as being reduced to a state of (almost) sheer biological existence, and their release was presented less as the beginning of a new *life* outside prison and more as the possibility of a dignified *death*.

Twenty applicants emphasized that their punishment not only destroyed their physical well-being but also eroded their social identity and connectedness to others, resulting in what they described as a form of "social death": "I know nowhere aside from prison; I have destroyed my life" (case-59207-06-16). They highlighted the loss of parenthood or marriage caused by long-term imprisonment: "I have no family, I am helpless" (case-28965-11-15) or "My marriage was destroyed" (case-4865-04-21). These applicants also described a sense of "biographical rupture" in their lives, attributing the rupture to their prolonged incarceration, which had consumed the majority of their adult years (Crewe et al., 2020). They conveyed a kind of self-eulogy in which they lamented their shattered and wasted lives, mixing depression and a realistic acceptance of their status:

> I am an elderly [person], with no direction for my future; I use drugs to escape my painful reality. All my friends from my childhood neighborhood are married, with children, and I sit all the time, thinking about how I live without a purpose, falling into an endless abyss. (case-12104-06-18)

For some applicants, their perceived social death was closely tied to the anticipated challenges they would face after release: "If you release me to the street, like a cat, I'll have no idea what's going on outside ... for me, it'll be a new world" (case-26776-03-22).

The applicants were acutely aware of their stigmatization, which they perceived as being "mirrored" back to them through both prison life and society (Ievins, 2023): "I look all the time at other people around me as injurious people, hostile, the worst; when I look in the mirror I see the same" (case-31992-02-22) or "I'll have a stain my whole life after what I did" (case-53261-10-21). They further argued that even if released they would continue to face stigma and significant challenges in finding employment, housing, or new relationships: "Because of my stigma, I will need to move to another place" (case-55058-01-16).

Through these narratives, the applicants sought to convey that their punishment had become equivalent to death by incarceration. Thus, they argued that even if released, they were irreparably broken and could not return to their pre-punishment biological or social condition.

Making Room for Self-punishment

Sixty applicants presented to the board a transformed, desisting self, drawing on themes recognized in reintegrative shaming (Makkai & Braithwaite, 1994), desistance (Maruna, 2001), self-presentation (Goffman, 1971), and post-traumatic growth theories (Crewe et al., 2020). Prison rehabilitation, according to these narratives, had allowed applicants to humanize themselves, find a listening ear, express themselves in a way that was not centered on the murderer stereotype, and make themselves believe they were morally "redeemable," as has been found in other "redemption narrative" contexts (Maruna, 2001):

> The people who lifted me up in the prison system and the amazing social workers brought me here ... I'll never forget these social workers who brought me to the point that I could dive deep inside myself to see where I went wrong and what thoughts I had. [They] re-educated me ... because of the social workers I opened my heart, I'm not ashamed to say things, they gave me the feeling I could talk about what hurt me. (case-53991-03-19)

These applicants described how they had "knifed off" (Laub & Sampson, 2003) their old, "false," negative lives in favor of a new, "true," positive existence:

> Today I am a different person, I can work and function like any honest citizen in every way, I have changed, I have matured, I have internalized, I have learned lessons and I have chosen a path for myself, I have chosen the path of righteousness ... I have changed, and I am committed to living a better life. (case-12104-06-18)

The process of "splitting" between their past and present selves was described by these applicants as slow and uneasy, often attributed to the corrections officers' efforts (Goffman, 1971): "This change took me 19 years; I didn't build myself overnight, but slowly through hard work" (case-12104-06-18). These applicants identified significant "turning points" in their lives: "After half of my sentence I was mature, became sane, and understood my acts" (case-13842-08-14). Portraying themselves as changed moral individuals, these applicants described themselves as "good," "humane," "reliable," "mature," "responsible," and "reformed" as is common in "redemption narratives" of ex-offenders (Maruna, 2001) (Grace, 2022):

> I was in solitary [confinement] for about 10 years ... I was problematic and transferred to another prison ... then, I joined my first [rehabilitation] group. From that point, I started to understand things, the group facilitators shaped me, gave me self-awareness, and taught me how to control my anger ... I murdered cruelly and did terrible things (crying), but back then I was one person, and now I am someone else. Once I was an animal, but after years, something started to "cook" in me, to sober up, to understand my acts. (case-13842-08-14)

As expected, these applicants expressed a deep sense of remorse, contrition, and self-condemnation, consistent with findings in similar correctional contexts (Weisman, 2009; Young & Chimowitz, 2022). Some applicants conveyed general remorse to the board, expressing regret for "what I have done," the "incident," "act," "lifestyle," or for "those whom I have harmed." Mostly, however, their remorse was directed personally toward the SVs: "I want to take advantage of the deceased's family being here; for 22 years I have been waiting to tell them that I understand their pain" (case-47246-06-20). These applicants also acknowledged the unlikelihood of receiving forgiveness from the SVs, given the severity of their crimes: "[The] parents will not forgive me. If I were in their place, I wouldn't forgive myself either" (case-30749-10-21).

A key aspect of these remorseful expressions was the portrayal of the applicants' inner pain (31 applicants). In these moments, the focus of moral engagement shifted inward and toward deep regret over their own perceived inner immorality. Seeking to make their invisible pangs of guilt visible, the applicants' performance of remorse often involved crying and displays of brokenness and self-loathing:

> This is a crime (crying) that is very hard ... I can't handle the thought that I caused the death of [victim's name], it is still hard today ... my whole life this has been hard for me, I can't sleep at night. I will never forgive myself ... no one can understand my pain, the suffering that I endured, it's endless. (case-11321-03-16)

These applicants' sense of the "moral weight" of their crime was described as a static and unchanging inner punishment, remaining unaffected by any personal changes during imprisonment or potential post-release, as has been found by scholars (Crewe et al., 2020). Importantly, such self-punishing pangs of guilt were described as something that would extend beyond the conclusion of their formal punishment: "My *punishment is much greater than imprisonment*; my punishment is with me every day" (case-63374-06-22) or "I'll carry this [pain] with me to the grave and I don't even know what awaits me after I leave this world (crying)" (case-49910-02-23).

Some applicants even inflicted permanent physical "stigmata" on themselves as a way to ensure their crime would never be forgotten: "I was afraid that I would forget what I did ... so I stubbed out a cigarette on my shoulder so it would always remind me ... the scar is here and also in my mind, and will be with me my whole life" (case-28683-11-19). Mirroring the SVs' narratives (sec. 5.2.1.), the dissonance between the applicants' continued lives and the unlived lives of their victims served as a constant reminder of their guilt: "The hardest thing for me is to see my children grow up and at the same time look at the victim's family" (case-53991-03-19).

Consumed by a sense of guilt, some applicants, particularly lifers, described inflicting real or imagined pain upon their bodies as signifying their atonement. Five applicants recounted suicide attempts, which they viewed as manifestations of their enduring guilt, particularly during the initial, most distressing period of their imprisonment. Others expressed a martyr fantasy, wishing to sacrifice their lives in exchange for the imagined resurrection of the victim:

> I don't have the will to live anymore ... I've lost 15 kilos, I wanted to end my life ... I tried to ask the [SVs] for forgiveness. Every time I saw them, I said: 'I wish it was me and not your son,' so that my mom and dad would cry for me and not his parents [for theirs] ... This is with me and will continue to be with me for the rest of my life ... it's still inside my heart and will stay until the grave. It will not end in prison ... I can't sleep without pills ... I ask God to take me, and then they will be happy and forgive me. (case-40665-02-22)

By portraying their inner suffering as omnipresent, the applicants presented themselves as moral and able to identify with and mirror the SVs' pain. Furthermore, because of such voluntary inner pain, they could be released from formal punishment, to "make room" for their informal self-imposed retribution, which was more severe and never-ending.

Punishment and Memory

Finally, the applicants connected their pangs of guilt to the memory surrounding the deceased. The applicants and their counsel usually acknowledged the status of SVs as being beyond dispute, often describing it as sacred: "The deceased's family statement is sacred, with no dispute, and it is naturally right; this is our starting point" (case-54100-03-19).

Seven applicants conveyed how they not only *respected* but had *internalized* the memory of the victims. Such a narrative is in line with the retributive notion that punishment is a moral way to keep faith with the victim and honor their memory for future generations (Ignatieff, 2000). What these applicants sought was to break the link between memory and suffering. They described how they carried the burden of memory and strove to preserve and reproduce the victim's memory for future generations. They argued that they were symbolically, emotionally, or physically engaged with the absent victims, positioning themselves as active "memory workers" dedicated to preserving their victims' memory both in prison and, if released, in the outside world (Kidron, 2003). For some applicants, this memory work took place within prison cells: "I have an electric memorial candle [for the victim] in my cell (crying); even if I'm released this will be with me for the rest of my days" (case-61872-02-18). Others wrote symbolic letters to their deceased victims, prayed for their memory, or visited their graves during furloughs: "I have already visited his grave and asked for his forgiveness. I will continue to pray for his family" (case-1476-05-17). Some applicants also pledged to construct physical or symbolic memorials for their victims upon their release: I want to build a monument to [the victim's memory] in the place where I took his life. I will work hard for this my whole life. Every year I will do a memorial service for him in the synagogue. I will dedicate myself to helping young children. (case-62820-07-21)

As the applicants took on the role of memory workers for their victims, they implicitly suggested that further formal punishment was unnecessary for embodying the victims' memory in reality. Furthermore, the applicants emphasized that their guilt could be addressed not only through passive suffering but also through active acts of atonement and memory within the law-abiding community. Finally, this narrative indicates that despite their identity "split" between past and present, they did not dissociate completely from their criminal past. The enduring thread of memory underscores their identity continuity from the past through the present into their future.

5.3.3 Moral Character "Bookkeeping"

Applicants transitioned from reconstructing their crime to reflecting on their moral character, emphasizing their "ethical selfhood" despite their crimes (Crewe et al., 2020). They revisited their overall life histories, presenting a moral "ledger" in an attempt to balance, at least to some extent, the immorality of their crimes (Maruna & Copes, 2005). The aim of such work was to manage their degraded moral identity, arguing that their "stained" criminal "master status" as homicide offenders did not fully capture their moral, or even ethically virtuous, potential (Goffman, 1963/1986).

Acknowledging that their actions had radically deviated from community values, applicants sought to counterbalance this deviation by showing that they had engaged in extraordinary acts of selflessness before their imprisonment:

> I helped for many years, especially as a nurse in the army hospital and also in the army ... In my army [service], I went above and beyond. I was sinking in the sea at war ... I found myself in the water and helping people and whoever was near me, I didn't leave, I helped time and again. (case-25827-08-14)

For several applicants, saving lives was achieved through voluntary work in prison, such as preventing their fellow prisoners from committing suicide or falling into drug addiction: "I was a volunteer in a juvenile prison ... [I] saved at least four boys from suicide" (case-1920-02-18). These proactive efforts represented active acts of moral payback, where applicants harnessed their profound sense of guilt as a motivating force rather than allowing it to paralyze them, encouraging them to make amends: "All sorrow and pain I feel, shame and remorse, it is with me every day. I chose to volunteer, to atone for what I did, to feel that I did something good in this world" (case-11529-02-22).

Other applicants extended their life-saving acts to plans for their post-release stage, emphasizing their ability to offer first aid as a symbolic means of balancing out their crime: "[I] enrolled in a first aid course ... to save lives. *This will not bring the deceased back but will compensate society and others for [my] acts ... by life-saving acts*" (case-9913-03-18). Several applicants further argued that upon release they would dedicate themselves to saving the lives of individuals facing mental health challenges:

> I have done a lot of bad things ... [but] I do have the potential to help and make amends for the things I have done ... [I] can support prisoners with psychiatric conditions ... a person like me who has harmed others can potentially save lives. (case-15008-07-20)

Several applicants expressed that their postrelease lives would be dedicated to caring for their own loved ones, such as spouses, children, or grandchildren who needed support: "Please allow me to take care of my mom, who is unfortunately sick with cancer" (case-15883-10-23). A common form of payback, aligning with future-oriented generativity-oriented "redemption scripts" (Crewe et al., 2020; Maruna, 2001), was a commitment to educating future generations:

> I can amend my future and the future of other youths who didn't have anyone to take care of them and help them. I know this is my future, helping at-risk youth, amending what I cannot amend for myself. (case-31357-07-21)

Finally, applicants stressed that they shared a moral-social world with law-abiding citizens; they had gained insight into their faults and personal shortcomings and had acquired a morally responsible and socially beneficent orientation. They highlighted their participation in work-release programs, where they collaborated with law-abiding citizens and earned their trust and appreciation, suggesting that the boundary between themselves and society was "reversible" (Herbert, 2024): "I go to work every day; I ask myself, does anyone even know that I am a convicted murderer?" (case-1920-02-18). To reinforce this integration, applicants or their counsel listed their "social rewards" (James & Gossett, 2018), such as professional or educational credentials earned, as evidence of their productive and moral character:

> There are certificates [submitted to the board] ... participation in various projects, in education ... classes, matriculation exams that were completed in prison, participation in the Remembrance Day ceremony ... Integration into society at the end of the day is also these things ... *It's symbolic, these things.* (case-12104-06-18)

Relatedly, the applicants emphasized their strong community ties in contrast to their weak connection to the criminal world: "I have been disconnected from criminals for 11 years ... my wife, my children, and my mother are my friends ... I have no friends in prison ... when I see criminals today there is not even a 'Hi' between us" (case-44811-08-18). Applicants also stressed how their relatives and friends trusted them and could serve as "personal vouchers" for their morality (Maruna, 2011): "My wife said to me: 'I'm with you until the end. I know who you are, a good person'" (case-49910-02-23). As such, applicants expressed that their moral-social status could easily reversed or had already been reversed, as they had never truly ceased being part of the law-abiding community, being essentially "insiders," and held a close "distance" from the community (Becker, 1963). In sum, applicants' moral labor focused on managing their profound sense of guilt through revisiting the moral meaning of their past crime, reconstructing their punishment severity from the perspective of the present, and conducting moral character bookkeeping that spanned their past, present, and future.

5.4 "This risk assessment depends on a values-based criterion": The Moral Labor of Parole Boards

The board concluded the hearings with its decisions, following deliberation among its members. As noted, the release rate was on average 26.2% for murder cases and 39.8% for manslaughter cases. The board emphasized that parole release was far from guaranteed, particularly given the severity of their crimes and the SVs' resistance: "A prisoner must serve the sentence imposed by the court and does not have an inherent right to early release" (case-55097-05-19) and "We can understand that the victims' parents wish to see the prisoner fully serve his sentence" (case-13383-11-20). As such, what did it take for the board to morally justify parole? The board offered two ways to do so, choosing to set its cursor either as distant from the court and sentencing justice (echoing the work of prison correctional officers) or as complementary to the court and sentencing justice.

5.4.1 Reaffirming Correctional Work: From Neoclassical to Positivistic Justice

One way to morally justify parole is to acknowledge that it reflects a distinct penological and institutional framework separate from retributive sentencing. The board does not debate the morality of retributive sentencing; instead, it expresses the benefits of utilitarian and positivistic penology. This narrative, commonly invoked in cases of parole *release*, involves "boundary work" (Gieryn, 1983) that demarcates the positivistic parole from the neo-classical-retributive sentencing: "The question that stands before us today is not a question of punishment but whether we can allow parole" (case-17998-07-17) and "The parole process is future-looking" (case-22792-08-19). Thus, the board's discretion is individualized, and the expertise of correctional officers is paramount, as they possess "the clinical experience and training" for promoting public safety and reintegration (case-18096-08-17). Such officers are "closely connected to the prisoner" and "have experience," as noted by the board in several cases. The shift from judicial to clinical expertise introduces three transformations of neoclassical sentencing vocabulary and logic.

First, *parole is in the "public interest."* The AGRs, providing the judicial narrative, framed the prioritizing of punitive public messages as being in the "public interest" (sec. 5.1.1.): "The public interest, beyond rehabilitation, is deterrence ... a public message should come from the board: [Those] who take lives ... must know that they have to pay the price to society" (case-31357-07-21). In contrast, to allow parole, the board in seven cases interpreted the "public interest" as being rooted in the promotion of public safety through correctional intervention. The "benefit to society" lies in the conditional release of the applicants, who are prepared to reintegrate as "loyal citizens" under the guidance and supervision of correctional officers:

> A prisoner being released after such a long incarceration must undergo a process of reintegration. A returning prisoner occasionally encounters difficulties, which they can overcome only with the help of correctional officers who will assist them during their adjustment period. Such assistance benefits society as a whole, as it will help return the prisoner to civilized society as a productive and loyal person. The alternative is to continue imprisonment to the end, as the state requests, so that eventually they will be released without any support to assist and supervise them in their first steps. (case-17620-06-14)

The attention is thus shifted to the correctional officers, who promote utilitarian rather than retributive values. Such correctional officers offer a different kind of expertise that promotes public safety in a way that a punitive approach cannot allow.

Second, *parole serves as a limit on punishment severity*. From the board's perspective, in thirteen cases, the shift from neoclassical to positivistic penology allowed applicants to enjoy the benefits of the "calm reason" of rehabilitation rather than suffer the "passionate heat" of vengeful sentiments expressed by the AGRs and the SVs (Locke, 1690/1988, p. 262). As the board admitted during a moment of disclosure:

> The deceased's mother asks [us] to consider the severity of the act [and] its cruel and unforgivable manner ... this is a brutal and senseless death that shocked the entire public. *However, it is pertinent to inform the mother that the board's discretion is governed by a well-defined legal set of considerations that constitute the foundation of its decisions.* That said, we are compelled to confess, with utmost candor, that as we sign the release order, our hands tremble, and our hearts pound with profound disquiet, as the prisoner has violated, *with callous disregard and unparalleled barbarity, the most sacred universal value – even if it has no basis in law – the sanctity of life*. (case-41927-03-16)

Here, the board's commitment to positivistic logic acted as a restraint on the punitive emotions of the SVs and the public, even when universal moral principles might demand parole rejection for especially serious cases of murder. The board's discretion here was firmly grounded within and for the service of the rule of law – which reflects the utilitarian aims of risk-reduction and rehabilitation – rather than undermining it. Relatedly, acting under positivistic logic, the board was willing to accept the applicants' remorse (if viewed as sincere) even when the SVs rejected such remorse, transforming the meaning of such remorse from a private act to a public act governed by legal standards for promoting public safety.

Third, *rehabilitation, rather than punishment, must be exhausted*. Under a retributive framework, *penal time* must be fully served before release in order to "*exhaust* the law ... via the prisoner's serving his full sentence" (case-20798-11-17). In contrast, the board's positivistic approach emphasized in forty-three cases that *rehabilitation efforts*, rather than the mere passage of time, should have been fully exhausted before parole was granted:

> The question of whether the prisoner is worthy of release largely depends on the process that the prisoner has undergone during imprisonment ... When carefully examining the therapeutic process he has undergone in the last ten years, *the impression is that it has been an exhaustive rehabilitative-therapeutic process.* What more can be done for the prisoner's rehabilitation within prison walls? (case-51347-08-17)

Thus, after exhausting all rehabilitative possibilities, as determined by correctional officers' assessments, the release of rehabilitated applicants becomes essentially a *right*. Tellingly, the boards often frame successful applicants as being *fit* for parole, due to their exhaustion of rehabilitative possibilities and risk reduction. The board acts as an enforcer of such rights, and in the event of release, reaffirms and authorizes the work and value of correctional officers: "The prison rehabilitation officials deserve praise, and are full partners in the prisoners' success in deserving release" (case-24713-05-17) and "She underwent a long and extensive process of rehabilitation ... it can be said that her release was achieved ... through great effort and was granted by *right and not by grace*" (case-71571-04-18). The board thus constructs the denial of parole not as a success but as signifying the criminal justice system's (CJS's) failure to rehabilitate a prisoner even after decades within the prison system. As such, criticism regarding the immorality of parole should, actually, be directed at correctional officers rather than at the board (Bandura et al., 1996). Parole release implicitly validates, even praises, the work of correctional officers.

5.4.2 Doing Late Justice

Context-Sensitive Proportionality

The board's proportionality assessment is based on two judicial tools: "balancing" and "precedents." The board can deviate from the classic straightforward implementation of parole factors, "weighing" and "balancing on scales" the relevant considerations, as in judicial decision-making (McFadden, 1987).

For example, the board can try to strike a balance between retributive and rehabilitative considerations: "The offenses are of great severity, which outweighs the rehabilitation process that the prisoner has undergone" (case-15677-05-19). In a court-like way, the board also "distinguishes" between cases based on their severity, by using prior parole decisions submitted by the parties, which serve as "precedents." For example, the board distinguished between the applicant's case and that of another applicant (T.), based on their different crime severity:

> The applicant's counsel argued that T., convicted of driving under the influence of alcohol, killing a 13-year-old boy, was granted parole . . . . [But] the board believes that it is not possible to have an equal ruling for the applicant and T.'s case . . . as in our case, the prisoner has served [only] eight and a half years . . . punitive considerations are most critical in severe offenses with long sentences (case-15677-05-19).

In order to justify release, in line with applicants' narratives (sec. 5.3.1.-5.3.2.), the board individualized the retributive meaning of the applicants' *crime* and *punishment*.

In terms of *individualizing the crime*, the board made distinctions between different types of murder based on the question of culpability, providing nuance for the murder label. For example: (a) There were fourteen cases of *mental impairment* that did not meet the trial standard for an insanity defense or for diminished culpability-based sentencing mitigation: "Before the crime, the prisoner stopped psychiatric treatment . . . Her mental state deteriorated; delusional thinking was at the root of committing the crime" (case-28683-11-19); (b) there were fourteen cases of *young age*: "Given his relatively young age at the time of the crime . . . his judgment was not sufficiently developed. In light of his hardships, there is room to exercise a somewhat lenient judgment despite his severe and unacceptable act" (case-41810-12-18); and (c) there were three cases of *battered women who killed*: "Her background was characterized by severe and constant abuse [by the victim] which she internalized into her personality . . . she decided to rid of her husband, in a relationship that was forced upon her" (case-38017-08-18).

In terms of *individualizing the punishment*, the board might balance the seriousness of the crime with the severity of the punishment as emerged from applicants' "pains of imprisonment" narratives. The board considered the applicants' excessive prison hardship under three sets of circumstances: (a) there were four cases of *foreign applicants* who had limited access to furloughs, visitations, or treatment due to language barriers, and for them "prison conditions are more complex and difficult than those of other prisoners" (case-20370-06-16);

(b) there were two cases of *long periods in solitary confinement*, with such applicants being subject "to different conditions than are regular prisoners" (case-31992-02-22); and (c) there were twenty-nine cases of *severe medical conditions* (that did not justify medical parole), such as kidney or eyes diseases, and such prisoners "deal with complicated bodily suffering" (case-55097-05-19).

In sum, the board promoted justice, being the judge of both crime and punishment at the back-end of the CJS continuum. The board built a scale of moral "deservingness" of parole, indicating that certain murders were "not as bad" as others. The board also built a scale for the deservingness of punishments based on prison experience.

Penal Resonance: Echoing Censure over Time

The board's individualization work was not undertaken solely for the purpose of justifying parole. In particularly severe cases – such as the murder of a child, murder that murder that had been thoroughly premeditated or cases involving multiple victims – the board acted as a "re-sentencing" authority, a role found in several U.S. jurisdictions (Aviram, 2020). In twenty-nine cases, the board demarcated the immorality of different types of murder, individualizing the blanket message of mandatory life sentencing, and describing its role as "social-moral" (case-38419-01-19). In these cases, the board explicitly rejected parole as it wished to "promote general deterrence and preserve the public trust, even when the prisoner's characteristics and risk factors might otherwise justify parole" (case-38419-01-19). The board emphasized that such punitive parole denials serve to counter the "wrong message to society that human life does not have a great value" (case-61169-07-18) and "give due weight to the sanctity of life" (case-14782-07-19). In these severe cases, in line with the AGRs' narratives (sec. 5.1.1), the board constructed an "intertextual dialogue" (Eco, 1985) between sentencing and parole. By paraphrasing or directly quoting sentencing remarks, the board intertwined the narratives. Parole punitive discretion thus was legitimized as a continuation of the original censure, rather than an illegitimate act of out-of-court justice:

> [T]his murder shocked the entire country with its barbarity ... The sentencing remarks describe a premeditated murder: "It was murder for the sake of murder. An act of cruel and abominable wickedness. Without motive, a trace of reason, contour, a shred of mercy, or hesitation. Just like that, in the evening of a day, in a pastoral neighborhood of a city." The board believes this is a heinous, inhumane, and incomprehensible case of exceptional severity ... Our hearts bleed, and our eyes weep as we read the detailed judgment

of the court, describing in every detail the horror perpetrated by the prisoner. (case-41927-03-16)

Through such a re-censuring message, the board *echoed* the court's original condemnation, years after sentencing, reflecting on the enduring aftershocks of the crime on the community's sentiments and on the victim, resisting any claim that censure is no longer "fitting" over time (Na'Aman, 2020). The applicants, SVs, and broader public were repeatedly confronted with the moral "resonance" of the social trauma caused by the crime even decades later:

> This case involves the senseless and brutal murder of a young child, demonstrating a loss of humanity. The case of [the child's name], of blessed memory, *is etched in the Israeli collective memory for eternity*, and it can be said that even 39 years after it occurred, the level of abhorrence and disgust at the acts has not diminished. (case-22214-08-14)

The board thus offered a moral education to the public at large, suggesting that in very serious cases penal censure is static and immune to the passage of time. In such cases, the "collective memory" requires further censure to inform and reinforce the core values of the community (Durkheim, 1893/1997):

> Public trust in the judicial system is of paramount importance, and the public interest in deterring serious crimes holds great value. In cases where offenses that show a serious moral deficiency have been committed, parole may significantly undermine public trust in the judicial system and the deterrent purpose of criminal law. (case-1813-11-19)

The board, however, was careful to demarcate the preservation of public trust in the CJS from "parole populism" that would render the board's decisions illegitimate and emotive (Annison & Guiney, 2022). The board was aware that in homicide cases, negative public opinion was the rule: "All crimes of the kinds that were conducted by the prisoner are severe and naturally can raise a public outcry, and are punished severely by law" (case-17620-06-14). To tame the use of "harm to public trust" for parole denial, the board interpreted this "test" as *normative* rather than *empirical*, and as protecting primarily the moral integrity of courts:

> The test of the serious act requires caution and even great caution. It should be remembered that *"public trust" is not just an empirical matter but a normative issue in essence*. This means that it is appropriate to give weight to the public's possible reaction to parole only when that reaction reflects *the norms of the legal system* and expresses justified deterrence. (case-22214-08-19)

Thus, the board even declined a request to reject parole for an applicant convicted of murdering a police officer. Rejecting parole, in this case, would have been an act of retribution, considering the time already served by the applicant, and would thus not have met the *normative* criteria of "harm to public trust":

> We are satisfied that for someone who served more than 90% of his sentence ... his release will not severely harm the public trust ... The police position, principally resisting releasing police officers' murderers, *is too general and against the law*, considering that the prisoner served 32 out of 35 (case-13842-08-14)

The board also stressed the exceptionality of punitive discretion, suggesting that it should be saved for cases of "especially severe moral deficiency" (case-24850-01-22), "motivated by an ideological element" (case-17620-06-14), or "severe and inconceivable circumstances of the crimes" (case-22214-14).

The board thus justified cases of punitive discretion as completing and individualizing sentencing justice. By doing such work, the board sought to preserve the judiciary's legitimacy rather than to perform an emotive penal populism. By extending sentencing morality, the board was legitimized as a back-end court, giving nuance to sentencing justice and thus serving rather than undermining retributivism.

5.4.3 Placing Character on Trial

Alongside examining the crimes, the board also assessed the applicants' character, which became a main focus in its decision-making process. The board emphasized that the "main consideration" was the applicants' risk to public safety, aligning with the law and parole jurisprudence cited periodically in its decisions (case-26098-03-15). The board emphasized that risk was of particular importance in homicide cases. In such cases, there was a "presumption of dangerousness" (case-13842-08-14), and "the more serious the crimes, the greater the risk" (case-55097-05-19). However, the board did not merely conduct a clinical or actuarial assessment to determine the applicants' level of risk. Instead, it

placed the applicants' character on trial, evaluating whether their character had crossed the "moral threshold" for reintegration into society as returned citizens (Hawkins, 1983). To do so, the board, with the assistance of correctional clinical data, constructed the moral meaning of (a) *risk assessment,* (b) *victim recognition,* (c) *prison obedience,* and (d) *"insight."*

The Normative Meaning of Risk Assessment

The board very rarely defines its risk theory. In practice, the board offers several levels of risk that can be raised or lowered according to its discretion (Hawkins,

1983), such as requiring "risk elimination," "risk reduction," "risk minimization," "lack of risk," "risk that could be managed," or "satisfactory decreased risk." The board also does not define the type of risk assessed (e.g., technical violation of parole conditions or new crime), its outcome (e.g., re-conviction or re-incarceration), the period assessed (e.g., during the license period or even after the sentence), or the weight given to psycho-diagnostic, clinical, or actuarial risk assessment, in its decisions.

The board views risk in a hybrid way, as an amalgamation of moral, clinical, and actuarial assessments of needs and risk (24 cases) (Hannah-Moffat, 2013; Werth, 2017). Such hybrid risk theory includes *normative and values-based elements*:

> Risk to public safety is assessed on *values-based criteria* and is evaluated on the basis of the totality of data from the past to the time of decision-making ... This is reflected in the extent of the internalization of the lesson, *the recognition of the normative value violated by the prisoner*, the admission of guilt, sincere remorse, admitting to and abandoning the wrongdoing, the efforts made to amend the situation and to provide appropriate compensation to the victim. (case-2227-04-22)

The board's assessment encompasses the applicants' overall life course and utilizes all types of "character evidence" from law enforcement, correctional officers, and legal sources (Lacey, 2016). The risk/character assessment often begins in childhood: "The prisoner from early childhood absorbed harsh and difficult criminal values into his personality" (case-17636-05-16) or "Impulsivity, displacement of responsibility, social alienation, and rebelliousness characterized him in his youth ... and have been ingrained into his personality" (case-41810-12-18). When judging applicants' character, the board gives special attention to their crime and its immorality, couched in sensational language, often with the addition of applicants' criminal history: "[He] took the life of the deceased in an animalistic manner that the soul abhors, in a despicable way for which words cannot adequately express the villainy of the act that the prisoner committed" (case-1920-02-18). Applicants' character is also explored through their conduct during the criminal process: "Throughout criminal proceedings, from the police interrogation, [she] didn't take responsibility ... and she didn't seem bothered by her conscience" (case-15883-10-23). Such character judgments are stated in terms such as: "[His] essence reflects violent patterns" (case-55097-05-19) or "Criminality is deeply rooted within him" (case-13032-07-18). These hybrid character-risk judgments cut through positivistic and neoclassical discourses to arrive at a "values-based" assessment.

The Normative Meaning of Victim Recognition

The board placed a high rhetorical value on applicants' victim compensation, similar to that which occurs in several other jurisdictions (e.g., France) (Herzog-Evans & Padfield, 2015), expressing this sentiment explicitly (20 cases): "The board is very sensitive to the need for compensation for the victims" (case-69937-12-20). The compensation was so important that its payment was included in the license release conditions. The board also postponed the hearing time to allow applicants to pay at least a "symbolic sum" (case-74933-10-18):

> It is hereby clarified to the prisoner, for his understanding, that failure to pay even one payment can be grounds for revoking the license, and he knowingly waives any claim he has, or may have, that he cannot afford the mentioned amount unless it involves circumstances of force majeure. (case-38031-05-17)

The board regarded the compensation payment as more than mere compliance with the sentencing order. In fact, it served two key moral functions.

First, payment served *as evidence of "moral reform"* (McNeill & Maruna, 2010), demonstrating the sincerity of the applicant's "insight" into their crime and their internalization of its severity: "The payment of compensation is a very significant touchstone for the internalization of the insight (case-7514-11-20) or "Compensation is the clearest sign of remorse, repentance, and atonement" (case-30504-05-19). Conversely, the failure to provide compensation served as a "moral barometer" (Maslen, 2015), reflecting the authenticity of the applicants' *internal* moral labor: "the fact that he still has not paid at least part of the compensation indicates that his remorse is insincere and inauthentic" (case-59508-11-19). Put differently, the board performs a financial evaluation of the applicants' morality.

Second, compensation held a *relational* meaning, signifying recognition of the SVs' suffering, aligning with restorative justice scholarship (Daly & Proietti-Scifoni, 2011; Sharpe, 2013). Unlike the passive act of serving prison time, victim compensation was viewed as an active relational act made toward one's fellow citizen. Prison reform, the board (and AGRs) stressed, cannot be "engaging in some kind of *platonic process with yourself in some cave*, but being in interaction with the other, looking him in the eyes" (case-77504-12-20). Thus, failing to compensate the SVs showed the applicants' immorality, as such applicants "missed the opportunity to ease, at least minimally, the suffering caused" (case-28683-11-19). The board thus constructs the relational process of compensation to the SVs as evidence of the applicants' character improvement. The reformed character is measured and valued through solidarity and empathy with the wronged parties rather than through an isolated process.

The Normative Meaning of Prison Obedience

The board assessed whether the applicants' release was "appropriate" under the law (s.5), primarily through the lens of prison discipline, which functions as another tool for showing character improvement in some cases. Usually, the board's analysis of the applicants' disciplinary records was relatively "flat," brief, and technical, often limited to simply counting the number of infractions and noting their temporal proximity to the hearing: "Against the prisoner are four disciplinary offenses, the last one from 2019, and one deprivation of privileges" (case-19892-03-23). Rarely did the board reflect on the criminological meaning of the disciplinary infractions or the reasons behind them. Where the board delved into the implications of discipline (12 cases), it portrayed prison rules as intense, strict, and "tight," compared to the more relaxed norms of a community (Crewe et al., 2020). A violation of prison rules, however, put into question an applicant's ability to obey the norms of the community:

> The series of prison rules' violations by the prisoner ... teaches us that he did not adjust to the restrictions that were imposed on him, and thus it is hard to put trust in him that, if released, he will obey all the restrictions outside. (case-1441-05-17)

In some cases, the board demanded *perfect* obedience to prison rules as a prerequisite for earning its trust in an applicant's ability to conform to the law outside prison: "When a man causes harm to others barbarically and cruelly ... such a person should be released only when his prison conduct is *flawless*" (case-19975-07-22). Applicants who managed to achieve perfect compliance with prison rules were regarded as morally transformed and trustworthy. These individuals adhered to the strict and "hyper-legal" and harsh prison regime (Calavita & Jenness, 2015):

> Unlike most lifers we encounter ... he has served a long sentence of 33 years without a single disciplinary infraction ... prison conditions are harsh and stressful, and only a small number of prisoners can withstand them without violating prison's strict discipline ... the fact that a prisoner convicted of such serious and violent offenses, yet who has conducted himself so admirably within the prison walls ... suggests that he underwent a significant and genuine transformation. (case-17620-06-14)

In making this connection, even though the correlation between prison discipline and recidivism is unclear (Cochran et al., 2014), the board linked the normative significance of "law" both within and outside the prison. Good prison conduct was interpreted as evidence of moral transformation and a predictor of future compliance with a community's laws, given the inherent difficulty of adhering to strict prison rules.

The Normative Meaning of "Insight"

By law, the board should determine for lifers whether they "notably and tangibly changed in terms of understanding the severity of their acts" (s.10 (b)). This criterion has been quantitatively identified as one of the most prevalent (144 cases) and strongest predictors of parole release and was regularly applied by the board in the manslaughter cases analyzed. Throughout its decisions, the board referred to insight-related concepts such as "internalization," "guilt," "reflection," "responsibility-taking," "remorse," or "regret," and applicants were typically expected to develop such "insight" through correctional rehabilitation experts.

The board broadly defined the "notable and tangible change" requirement as "processing the criminal act, its reasons, results, and implications for the present and future ... taking responsibility for one's exact part in the crime and its meaning for present life and the future" (case-62363-12-18). The board also connected insight to the ability to control criminal impulses: "[the] development of mechanisms for responsibility, discipline, and internal boundary-setting" (case-33285-11-18). However, the board rarely analyzed the reasons behind an applicants' failure to demonstrate "insight," whether applicants lacked empathy, shame, a need to preserve a moral self-image or something else (Maruna & Mann, 2006; Piquero, 2017; Proeve, 2023; Tangney et al., 2014). The board also did not rely solely on correctional officers' insight assessment but took an active role in independently judging it (28 cases). In doing so, the board distinguished between merely "doing" insight and genuinely "being" insightful (Weisman, 2009): "Despite the correctional opinion regarding [his insight], the prisoner was given the right to speak before [us] ... apart from a long speech and stories ... we were struck that he didn't raise a hint of acceptance, regret, or empathy" (case-23536-02-18). The demonstration of "insight" was linked by the board to three moral purposes:

First, in line with applicants' narratives (sec. 5.3.2.), the board viewed their "insight" as reflecting a *painful identification with the harm caused by the crime*:

> We heard the prisoner himself, who spoke to us emotionally and at length. [He] expressed deep sorrow for the extensive harm caused by his act and did not try to minimize its severity. He agonized over the pain of the deceased victim's widow and children ... shed tears when talking about the pain he caused them (and sadly, the board's protocol cannot accurately convey what

we witnessed) ... we accept his expressions of regret, sorrow, and pain conveyed to us. (case-54185-05-16)

Without such painful insight, the board observed, the rehabilitation process becomes overly "sterile" and detached, lacking the necessary connection to the full relational meaning of the crime and the profound burden of causing immense suffering to others:

> What is the significance of a notable and substantial change ... when the prisoner denies committing the horrific crime he was convicted for? *He is not confronting the terrible act and its consequences ... he has undergone a largely "sterile" rehabilitation process that does not involve concrete engagement with the crime ... he has been spared the difficult and complex processing and internalizing of the legal proceedings and has been spared the need to deal with the suffering of the victim's family as the one who caused them this tragedy ...* The prisoner indeed shows empathy for the family's suffering but he does so as if he is not involved in the matter, when he is the one who caused that suffering. The difference between the two is profound. *The prisoner's denial has spared him the need to confront the difficult and burdensome legal truth that was established.* (case-17620-06-14)

Second, and in line with U.S. parole decision-making, the board rejected external explanations for the applicants' crimes, and required applicants to gain insight into themselves instead, constructing a *causal link between character and crime* (Shammas, 2019; Young & Chimowitz, 2022). Applicants were required to engage in deep soul-searching, where they confronted their "true" character as the source of their crime and hence their risk: "*He should delve into himself deeply*, so the full significance of the murder and its source will be understood" (case-63771-03-15). Similarly, the board ruled that an applicant who "is *not willing to face himself as he is* ... cannot be defined as someone who has undergone a significant and real change" (case-1162-05-18). The board criticized applicants who attributed their crimes to external factors: "He prefers circumstantial explanations for his problems" (case-2651-01-19) or "He finds difficulty in looking inside for the reasons for his violent choices" (case-55097-05-19). Truly insightful applicants, according to the board, could identify the cause of their crime within their character and demonstrate how they had learned to control their character flaws:

> The correctional staff emphasized that after the prisoner found his place in therapy ... began to open up and share his world honestly ... gained insight into his need for visibility, recognition and empowerment stemming from low self-esteem, and the emotional drivers behind his criminal world ... He understands that these needs still exist today, but he has learned that there are other ways to fulfill them that do not involve violence. (case-32028-05-20).

Such insightful applicants acknowledged the "nexus" between their character and their crime, and consequently, their risk (*In re Shaputis*, 2011). Furthermore, implicitly, through requiring insight, the board validated correctional work as a crucial tool in supporting applicants' moral improvement.

Third, the board linked applicants' "insight" to their *renewed commitment to shared social values*: "The prisoner's criminal consciousness has undergone a complete transformation into a healthy and amended *civic consciousness*" (case-38711-03-17). Insightful applicants, as "community members and citizens" (case-56041-09-16), were expected to acknowledge the judicial authority's legitimacy as a prerequisite for reintegration: "The prisoner might be ready to integrate into society ... However, such readiness is meaningless as it does not result from taking genuine responsibility and accepting his [the court's] judgment as true" (case-22214-08-14).

In sum, the board's construction of "insight" thus ensured that applicants could morally reflect upon their crime and had the inner capacity to act as moral agents autonomously and not just out of fear of the law. Relatedly, the board ensured that applicants understood the source of their crime to be from within their core selves rather than from external social forces or as being an out-of-character single failure. Successful applicants were viewed as those who could process, control, and manage their inner or external strains in a normative way. Furthermore, the board reaffirmed the court's judgments via the applicants' own words before their release, reinforcing the work of the courts as just and accurate (sec 4.1.2; Young & Chimowitz, 2022).

5.4.4 Closure, Agency, and Trust: Postrelease Supervision Hearings

The moral labor of the board extended beyond the decision to release applicants. Following their release, applicants – now parolees – were subject to the board's periodic assessment to evaluate their compliance with parole conditions (68 cases) (e.g., participation in treatment/work, regular reporting to the police). When necessary, the board adjusted parole conditions, either mitigating them (e.g., transferring parolees from a halfway house to private housing, removing electronic monitoring) or reinforcing them. Additionally, the board retained the authority to revoke the parole license if conditions were violated.

The periodic supervision hearings, conducted within local courtrooms, were typically brief and bureaucratic, often involving the submission of documents such as salary slips and reports from community correctional officers. However, these hearings also conveyed messages about the board's level of trust in the parolees' ability to navigate their post-release lives: "Clearly, we cannot allow [him] to move to a rented apartment; this is like putting an obstacle before a blind man" (case-3562-11-16) or "The prisoner has a lengthy parole period, and a certain level of supervision must be maintained throughout its duration" (case-19077-04-14). These hearings often included future-oriented warnings: "We warn the prisoner that he must fulfill all the release conditions and must not, heaven forbid, return to committing offenses. Any violation will bring him back before the board" (case-54185-05-16). That said, the hearings also provided an opportunity for the board to communicate positive messages of trust and encouragement in accordance with the parolees' progress: "We are impressed by the parolee who shows progress; the parolee is employed properly, earns his living with dignity, and provides for his family" (case-41810-12-18). The board acknowledged these successful parolees' efforts and potential to overcome re-entry challenges, reinforcing their progress toward reintegration (nine cases):

> We have heard from the prisoner about the challenges in her life, both in the health arena and in the family and employment arenas. It is understandable that after staying in a hostel, integration into the family involves difficulties. *We trust that the prisoner, thanks to her abilities and skills, will also overcome the hurdles in this area.* (case-17507-04-18)

In such cases, the board thus adopted a caring and supportive tone, signaling the closure of the parolees' previous criminal life and the beginning of a new law-abiding chapter. This message guided the transition from the liminal prisoner-to-citizen status. The board, in these cases, communicated and approved the parolees' new status as returning citizens who were not identical with their crime (Austin, 1979):

> Your employer is very satisfied, you're very committed to the project, and you're making the most of life outside [prison] in a good and quality way, and that's truly beautiful ... We congratulate the parolee for strongly standing by the release conditions and wish him continued success on his way. (case-28965-11-15)

The parolees' responses to these encouraging messages were also filled with gratitude, hope, and agency: "I thank the board for its trust in me" (case-56048-09-16), "Thank you for your support and the opportunity" (case-54100-03-19), or "I am happy to hear that the reports on me are positive; I was in a dark hole but now I have a family, and God willing, a child" (case-64765-01-19).

This process concludes the journey that began years earlier when the parolees were first held accountable for violating community values. At this stage, the board serves as the voice of the community, marking the closure of the criminal process. These successful parolees are seen as moral agents who, despite committing severe crimes, are not irredeemably criminal; their character has improved and they can be trusted to act in a law-abiding manner.

6 Revisiting Justice: Discussing the Moral Meaning of Parole

6.1 The Moral Laboratory of Parole

Decades after the crime, the moral "theatre" of parole is used by parole actors, each in their own "act" (Goffman, 1959/1980), alone or "co-authoring" with other narratives or texts (Maruna & Liem, 2021), to reinforce, revisit, and challenge the moral meaning of character, crime, and punishment.

The quantitative findings suggest, as shown, that retributive factors – related to crime and moral character – make a unique contribution to the variability in boards' decisions, beyond the traditional considerations of risk and rehabilitation. The qualitative analysis (see Figure 1) supports this interpretation, indicating that the board evaluates crime, punishment, and character through a broadly defined retributive lens, rather than exclusively through a risk-and-rehabilitation framework. We found that complex and possibly conflicting retributive discourses, both explicit and implicit, served as another "master frame" (Hawkins, 1983) for understanding parole. Viewed in this light, parole hearings function as a "laboratory" for examining how the fundamental components of character, crime, and punishment evolve. The distinct institutional setting of parole allows parole actors to reexamine the basic sentencing "substances" of character, crime, and punishment in light of the passage of time and the correctional process.

The moral meaning of character. The AGRs cast doubt on the coherence and morality of the applicants' character, being "others" both in utilitarian and retributive terms. The SVs framed the applicants according to their past crimes. The applicants, in contrast, attempted to reconstruct their core character as moral, improved, and having desisted, employing strategies such as stigma management, splitting, and moral bookkeeping. They also claimed that either their crime did not reflect their core character was committed in a moment of failure or as a result of external criminological forces, or that their character was flawed at the time of the crime but that this old character was long gone, and their new desisting character had evolved instead. The board, in effectively putting the applicants' character on "trial," engaged in a hybrid assessment of risk and moral character. This moral character assessment involved rewarding applicants' recognition of their victims, adherence to the rigid norms of prison life, and evidence of "soul work" through showing insight into their crimes. The board further ensured that the applicants did not just justify their crime as an out-of-character act but as deriving from their core character, which they could now control and manage. The board also showed that parolees were essentially moral in their postrelease lives and that their crimes had not deterministically defined them.

The moral meaning of the crime and punishment. The AGRs constructed a *static and past-looking* view of the applicants and their crimes, framing parole as a source of conflict with sentencing justice. According to this perspective, applicants were expected to internalize the judicial-moral messages, accept their remorse as morally required, reaffirm that their release was morally *undeserved*, and refrain from focusing on their own pains and challenges. Similarly, the SVs adopted a crime-focused narrative but emphasized a more personal account of the crime's ongoing harms. This approach highlighted the irreversibility and unforgivability of the crime, reinforcing the view that parole represents a moral threat to the CJS's commitment to do justice. The applicants' narratives can be viewed as a response to these arguments. To justify the morality of their release, applicants revisited key components of proportionality. First, they recontextualized the severity of their crimes, presenting them as part of a broader, time-expansive story rather than one point in time, which must be contextualized within broader criminological factors. Second, by reframing the severity of their punishment – describing their punishment as a "biological and social death" and expressing their own self-punishment – they rendered further punishment unnecessary. Finally, the board offered a balanced approach, aiming to individualize and contextualize proportionality to justify parole decisions. In some cases, doing so involved acknowledging the applicants' rehabilitation and readiness for reintegration. In other, particularly severe cases, the board re-emphasized censure, extending the moral work of sentencing over decades. This approach treated censure as a multitemporal process rather than a one-time act, allowing for both accountability and eventual reintegration.

6.2 Revisiting Theory: Theorizing the Moral Meaning of Parole

6.2.1 Explaining the Retributive Labor of Parole

The intensive and nuanced moral labor observed during parole hearings, which goes beyond "re-sentencing" (Vîlcică, 2018), invites explanation. I will argue that the moral meaning of parole that was found in the current study can be explained by the similarities between parole and sentencing hearings, the overlap between utilitarian and retributive assessment, and the possibility of filling the moral void of retributive sentencing through parole hearings.

Parole Hearing as a Back-End Court

The moral labor conducted in parole hearings may follow an "if it looks like a duck" logic. Despite its administrative label, parole involves sentencing-like features: the potential for significant reductions in prison time in case of release, the curtailing of applicants' hope for release after years behind bars in case of denial, and discretionary decision-making headed by a judge with legal actors. Parole actors thus treat parole hearings as what they functionally are: a judicial-like late sentencing process. Put differently, the moral-social sentiments toward crime and character do not vanish just because the label "in the books" of parole is utilitarian. Parole actors engage with the penal reality as it is rather than how the law imagines it.

The specific institutional and socio-legal context in Israel is particularly relevant here. The board operates under the judiciary branch (Judicial Authority, 2023) and functions within a predominantly retributive-oriented sentencing system (Roberts & Gazal-Ayal, 2013). The board's work has also been linked by courts to the broader functions of criminal law (*Doe v. Israel*, 2022), and the board is authorized to consider punitive factors in exceptional cases (s.10(a)). Finally, prison rehabilitation programs in Israel often emphasize moral-related themes (e.g., responsibility-taking), which may contribute to the alignment of the board's decisions with this correctional culture (Haviv et al., 2020). Future research is needed to confirm and further explore these dynamics.

The personal backgrounds of parole chairpersons as judges might impact their parole work, bringing their judicial "tool kit" (e.g., judicial tools of "balancing" and "distinguishing") and their sentencing philosophy to the parole process (Ruhland, 2020). In this regard, the observed moral labor of the board also reflects an "institutional isomorphism," whereby the board adopts judicial norms to gain legitimacy in managing the inherent uncertainties of risk prediction, reinforcing the legitimacy of its decisions through both retributive and utilitarian discourses (DiMaggio & Powell, 1983). It might be that such moral labor serves to increase the board's professional capital and identity vis-a-vis the correctional actors and the courts (Bourdieu, 1987). When conducting moral labor, the board is not just technically applying correctional officers' recommendations or undermining sentencing determinations. Instead, the board's moral labor suggests that it has its own moral agenda that is not only justified in its own right, but even reinforces, completes, and amends sentencing justice.

The Moral Dimensions of Risk and Rehabilitation

Risk assessment is often regarded by retributive theorists as being in "direct and obvious conflict with desert" (de Keijser et al., 2019, p. 3). However, the findings suggest that the boundaries between these concepts for parole actors are often fluid. The board, as shown, applied a broad and hybrid assessment of risk that spanned from the time of the crime to the court's assessment, including the entire prison phase and during the parole period (if released). Tracing the trajectory of a moral character for a long period ultimately embodies the inescapable moral dimensions inherent in assessing risk and rehabilitation. The board's broad and hybrid risk assessment in this way aligns with studies suggesting that risk assessment is an essentially moral judgement (Hannah-Moffat, 1999; Lynch, 1998; McNeill et al., 2009), that parole risk assessment is primarily past-looking (Pogrebin et al., 2015), and that retributive and utilitarian frameworks can be closely related in practice and in theory (Ball, 2011; du Bois-Pedain, 2024; Efodi, 2014; McNeill, 2012; Rotman, 2024).

The Pluralistic Nature of Retributivism

Nearly a century ago, Burgess (1936, p. 494) argued: "The failures of our entire system of criminal justice ... accumulate and become evident in parole." This critique can also be extended to the shortcomings of retributive sentencing, which might account for the moral labor of parole found in this study. Offering a more pluralistic retributive theory, parole hearings allow one to address the neglect of moral character, the (in)justice of crime judgments, and the indifference to the subjective experience of imprisonment under traditional retributive theory.

First, regarding *the neglect of moral character*, traditional retributivists regard offenders as rights-bearing agents who should be judged solely for their crimes rather than their character (Ashworth & Horder, 2013). However, ignoring offenders' character by focusing solely on their crime is morally problematic and shows an indifference to the extreme complexity and uniqueness of individual character (Smith, 2016) and the realistic possibility of character change with time (Crewe et al., 2020).

The neglect of character at sentencing ignores the fact that censure is imposed on *human beings*, not on *acts*, and that "our sense of justice requires us to consider the whole person" (Whitman, 2014, p. 148). Indeed, research suggests that the very possibility of ignoring human character when passing moral judgments is questionable, considering subconscious intuitions that capture both crime and character (Atari et al., 2023; Bartels et al., 2016; Slobogin & Brinkley-Rubinstein, 2013). Thus, the board's character-oriented moral labor possibly balances the neglect of character in the crime-oriented mandatory sentencing, completing the narrow view of sentencing through the back-end holistic judgment of parole.

Second, regarding *the perceived (in)justice of crime judgments*, in mandatory life sentencing all murder cases are treated equally, with any specific moral distinctions between acts that fall under the umbrella definition of "murder" being neglected. Such a sentencing policy harms proportionality and justice, mislabels crimes and offenders, and diverges from community views that individualize murder according to offenders' specific blame-worthiness

(Mitchell & Roberts, 2012; Robinson, 2012). This moral labor, therefore, may be seen as an effort to address the shortcomings of mandatory life sentencing, seeking to capture the nuances of murder not recognized by mandatory sentences – a proper respect of the ordinal ranking of proportionality. Such respect is achieved through echoing censure over time in especially severe murder cases, or by contextualizing murder within broader criminological contexts of strains, peer pressure, or poor social control. This notion may explain the parole actors' "talismanic" attraction to crime severity (*In re Shaputis*, 2011, p. 275).

Furthermore, the division of moral labor between sentencing and parole allows the CJS to capture the immorality of murder on different levels (Dan-Cohen, 1983). At the sentencing level, mandatory sentencing equally censures every unlawful intentional killing. At the parole level, however, the lower visibility of parole allows for a refinement of the judicial work in a more individualized way.

Relatedly, parole may serve as an antidote to the "silent" nature of mandatory sentencing. At sentencing, the parties are largely silent, with little opportunity to alter the sentence, and applicants may be emotionally overwhelmed in the face of their expected sentence (Schinkel, 2014). Thus, the moral labor operating at parole board hearings may help to address the communicative void caused by the "deafness" of mandatory sentencing.[29] During parole hearings, after years, the applicants can actively respond to the sentencing censure as ethical and morally reformed agents (Crewe et al., 2020; Jarman, 2020). In turn, they can "hear" the community's response to their "answer" through the reaffirmation of their agency and trust during post-release hearings. After all, reintegration – like sentencing communication – is a "two-way process" and cannot be fully achieved without society's recognition (McNeill, 2012; Maruna, 2011). This reciprocal process ideally marks the closure (or movement toward closure) of the penal dialogue that began at sentencing.

Third, regarding *the indifference to subjective experiences*, traditional retributivists often view sentencing as an "abstract" and "disembodied" assessment of censure, measured by *quantitative* units of liberty deprivation imposed by a *formal* court (Garland, 2011; Kolber, 2009). In contrast, applicants viewed their punishment as a *qualitative* painful experience. The pains of long-term imprisonment, as they viewed them, were bodily and socially destructive, in prison and even after release, for themselves and their families, and went well beyond liberty deprivation. They also viewed their punishment as including the pains of their *informal* self-imposed pangs of guilt (Harrison & Duff, 1988). For SVs, parole hearings allowed them to express more fully the private meaning of the

---

[29] Manslaughter offenders are often silent at sentencing, whether due to the reality of plea-bargain-based sentencing agreements or to the difficulty of accepting guilt in a public courtroom (Bibas, 2012).

crime that had taken over their lives. Looked at in this way, parole allow a more pluralistic retributive theory of punishment. If *public-objective* messages stand at the heart of sentencing, over time, the *private-subjective* meaning of punishment may also be considered through parole hearings.

In sum, the moral labor of parole reflects the "multi-vocal" nature of retributivism, which is multi-staged and pluralistic (Cottingham, 1979, p. 238). Parole pluralistic retributivism, from this perspective, requires methodological and conceptual shifts in what retributivism does and how it is measured over time. Such moral labor addresses key internal limitations of retributive sentencing – through a more dynamic, private, subjective, and morally diverse retributive theory.

6.2.2 Revisiting Penal and Criminological Theory

Penal Theory

The findings reflect a divide between how traditional retributivists conceptualize crime and punishment and how parole actors experience them. As seen, contrary to the tenets of traditional retributivism (von Hirsch, 2017), for example, parole actors adopt a broad timeframe of culpability, are morally character-oriented, and view penal suffering in qualitative terms.

Traditional retributivists might contend that the findings, at best, highlight the imperfections of penal reality (e.g., excessive prison suffering) rather than the deficiencies in retributive theory itself. Some may even contend that retributivism concerns only the determination of sentencing length and has no significance after the sentencing judge's gavel falls. However, even without fully resolving the complex relationship between retributive theory and reality, one should recall that retributivism has real-world implications – sometimes devastating – for people's lives (Hanan, 2020). Furthermore, retributive theory seeks to offer ethical guidance for practical decision-making and protect such decision-making from abuse (Ryberg, 2025). Thus, it seems reasonable to connect retributive sentencing to its intended and unintended effects on human beings during and after prison, including what retributivism does, to whom, where, and when. At the very least, retributivists should acknowledge any gaps between retributive ideals and their real-world application, taking these gaps into consideration when developing theory and appreciating its potential limits (Duff, 2010). Otherwise, retributivism risks losing its moral force to guide policy (Robinson & Holcomb, 2021) or might even be viewed as a form of legal "violence" rather than a moral way of doing justice (Cover, 1986).

A greater attentiveness by retributivists to the realities of prison, parole, and reentry is a key lesson from this study. Recent developments in homicide law in

Israel show the significance of this lesson. In 2019, a major legal reform in Israel, motivated by retributive values, individualized blame in homicide cases by legislating new homicide offenses (Penal Law, 1977 [2019]).[30] The reason for this reform, as stated in the bill (2015), was that the single category of "murder" was "excessively narrow, on the one hand, and excessively broad on the other" (p. 166; Kremnitzer Report, 2011). Although this reform did not affect the cases analyzed, the findings shed empirical light on it. As shown, parole actors expressed dissatisfaction with the unidimensional category of "murder" and attempted to introduce shades of color into the black-and-white framework of murder law. Parole actors believe that not all murderers are created morally equal; rather, they should be distinguished according to individual culpability, which should be more context-sensitive (e.g., the reasons for the crime). The findings support the need for the 2019 reform, at least from the parole actors' perspective. At the same time, the findings also raise questions for future studies: How parole hearings emerging from a more nuanced homicide law would look, and what kind of moral labor, if any, they would include.

Criminological Theory

The findings highlight the importance of revisiting prevalent criminological theories, such as the "new penology" (Feeley & Simon, 1992) or the "culture of control" (Garland, 2001), which have portrayed punishment administration as a phase of risk management, and as bureaucratic and devoid of moral, particularly retributive, significance (Kerr, 2019). In contrast to such portrayals, the findings suggest that parole hearings for homicides may function as a moral forum. In this way, the moral labor found to have been done by the board aligns with other examples of field-level actors who have deviated from a risk-management policy toward a more individualized, even moral, logic (Lynch, 1998; Maurutto & Hannah-Moffat, 2006).

The overall picture found here reinforces the "moral turn" in criminology and extends it to punishment administration work (Bottoms & Jacobs, 2023; Messner, 2012). The findings invite a more careful examination of the moral labor embedded within the ostensibly purely utilitarian process. Criminologists should engage to a greater extent with punishment administration practices through a moral lens, including the communicative, symbolic, and performative

---

[30] This includes: (1) "reckless manslaughter," carrying a maximum sentence of twelve years (s.301C); (2) "aggravated murder," an intentional or indifferent killing under severe circumstances, carrying a mandatory life sentence (s.300A); (3) "basic" murder, intentional or indifferent killing, carrying a maximum life sentence (s.300); and (4) "homicide with reduced responsibility," where the victim abused the offender and other mitigating factors, carrying a maximum sentence of fifteen years (s.301B; special provision for provocation).

moral discourses that take place within administrative and quasi-judicial bodies outside of courts, and how punishment administration authorities are connected to, echoed by, or resisted to the work of courts. For example, criminologists could take into consideration the moral dynamics of prison discipline and classification, community supervision, or reentry decision-making. In other words, criminologists must also be willing to engage to a greater extent with moral themes that are traditionally dominated by legal scholars, such as censure, atonement, repentance, or moral restoration, and their implications for criminological theory and policy. They should also offer a more nuanced metric for punishment administration work that measures its moral performance as well.

6.2.3 Revisiting Policy

The findings raise a difficult normative question: Should parole hearings be moral forum? After all, the board's expertise lies in rehabilitation and risk evaluation, but it may lack the legitimacy to pass retributive judgments (Ball, 2011). This study, as an empirical work, claims to solve this problem, touching on fundamental issues such as the relationship between time and punishment; sentencing and punishment administration; judicial and administrative decision-making; crime and character; individualism and equality; and more (du Bois-Pedain, 2019; Reitz, 2017). At the same time, the findings encourage policymakers to take more seriously how moral themes evolve over time after sentencing and what this evolution may imply for policy. The "journey" of moral labor across the CJS has meaning for perceived justice, fairness, and legitimacy, for both CJS actors and the public (Tyler, 2010). Although not offering magical solutions for these complex theoretical and practical issues, the following policy implications are suggested.

The AGRs' Role at Parole Hearings

As the findings suggest, the AGRs treat the hearings as an adversarial and punitive forum, evoking elements of a "disintegrative shaming" process (Makkai & Braithwaite, 1994). The traditional prosecutorial ethos is that of court-oriented, legal, and "crime-fighting" agencies (Green & Roiphe, 2020). Thus, the AGRs naturally construct the parole hearings as "legal combat" between themselves and the applicants who were convicted by law of serious crimes. The result is that parole rejection is viewed by the AGRs as a success (Dagan, 2023; Padfield et al., 2022). On these grounds, the AGRs' punitive and judicially-oriented approach requires rethinking under a future-looking parole process that seeks to promote re-entry and public safety. Even from a retributive perspective, it is unclear what new values the AGRs bring to the parole decision-making table by repeating the sentencing remarks for re-censuring the applicants' crime and character.

The rise of "community prosecution" or "progressive prosecution" in some U. S. jurisdictions demonstrates the possibility of a less adversarial and more problem-solving-oriented approach to prosecution parole work (Green & Roiphe, 2020; Murcia, 2022). Another alternative is for the state to be represented at parole hearings by probation or prison officers who are more oriented toward risk and rehabilitation (Hardwick, 2018; Ministry of Justice, 2022). In recent years, there has been a growing prosecutorial awareness in Israel of evidence-based policy, with efforts invested in alternatives to imprisonment (e.g., community courts) and a greater willingness to engage with public legitimacy (Dorner Report, 2015; Pedan, 2019; State Attorney, 2018). These shifts may signal a different future for prosecution involvement in parole work that is less punitive and more nuanced. Future research will help to confirm this notion.

The SVs' Role at Parole Hearings

The law emphasizes that victim impact statements (VISs) should focus on the expected risk of releasing a prisoner (s.19). However, consistent with previous studies, the SVs rarely added a risk-related value to the hearings. Instead, they expressed frustration about the perceived injustice of the CJS (Padfield, 2025; Riches & Dawson, 1998; Roberts & Erez, 2004) or they put pressure on the board to reject parole (Caplan, 2010; Hritz, 2021; Roberts, 2008). This reaction is to be expected, given the irreversible harm caused and the possibility of victims referring to the subjective emotions and impact of the crime (*State v. Ganame*, 2009). The following suggestions might make VISs more useful and less of a step in a never-ending cycle of resentment (Dhami, 2016).

First, parole for homicide cases holds significant emotional weight for SVs, as they involve deciding the liberty of those who killed their loved ones. However, as in other contexts, legal discourse is often opaque to laypeople (e.g., the definition of "life sentence") (Stygall, 2012). The SVs' understanding of the parole board's work is part of parole's (and possibly the CJS's) moral legitimacy. Therefore, the SVs should be provided with a basic understanding of what the parole decisions entail and their rationale, at least in broad terms. Of special importance is the relationship between the moral functions of sentencing and parole. In England and Wales, for example, SVs are instructed that the board "cannot consider whether it thinks further punishment is necessary" (UK Parole Board, 2015, p. 7).

Second, as the findings show, the moral labor of parole for SVs brings up emotional burdens and frustrations. Thus, SVs should be made aware of the benefits or drawbacks of testifying before the board, the possibly upsetting implications of parole release, and the fact that despite prison time possibly coming to an end, their pain will continue (Victims' Commissioner, 2024). Parole hearings can be an opportunity to identify the SVs' needs and frustrations, and direct them to legal and/or clinical counseling, restorative justice programs, or community health resources, in order to help them process their grief and address their financial and emotional needs (Caplan, 2012; Riches & Dawson, 1998; Padfield, 2025). These suggestions may help to alleviate some of the abovementioned concerns. Future research is much needed in this regard.

The Board's (and Applicants') Role at Parole Hearings

The Israeli board, like many parole jurisdictions in the United States and Europe (Rhine et al., 2017; van zyl Smit & Corda, 2018), is discretionary and holds authority to reevaluate all aspects of the original sentence. The board's assessment, as found, combines clinical, moral, and risk elements, raising concerns about inconsistent and potentially biased decision-making (Young & Pearlman, 2022). Given that the board *performs* retributive labor, and assuming that such work is desirable, parole criteria should reflect moral considerations transparently to ensure consistency and fairness, and achieve comparable outcomes (Hritz, 2021; Ruhland & Laskorunsky, 2025; Young & Pearlman, 2022). Transparent criteria and application are essential for advancing proportionality, an aim rooted in an equal distribution of justice. Punitive discretion in parole decision-making should be performed *cautiously*, as "it is easy for parole to become a re-sentencing exercise" (Padfield, 2025, p. 278). Another possibility to achieve proportionality is through parole guidelines for homicide cases, as seen in some U.S. jurisdictions (Rhine et al., 2017). Without exhausting this issue here, such guidelines could reflect the moral tensions that arise in homicide cases, including presumptive release dates that incorporate aggravating and mitigating factors in a way that balance both utilitarian and retributive values. In any case, applicants should be informed of what to expect at the hearing and the grounds on which their future freedom will be decided. At the very least, parole law should provide clarity regarding the real *threshold* for release either on risk or retributive grounds.

Furthermore, the moral labor found in this study raises a challenging question about how parole hearings *should be structured*. Some jurisdictions advocate for the judicialization of parole, at least in some respects (e.g., France, for reducing the minimum period to be served) (Herzog-Evans & Padfield, 2015). However, such judicialization excludes considerations of retribution and general deterrence from the parole decision-making (Herzog-Evans & Padfield,

2015). In the United States, a "second look" by a "judicial panel" was proposed by the drafters of the Model Penal Code, to allow the "modification" of long-term sentences on both retributive and utilitarian grounds (ALI, 2017, s.305.6).

The moral labor found in the current study suggests that parole hearings should be made public. Echoing censure over time or individualizing proportionality normally justifies open hearings. Even character judgments and reaffirmations of citizenship status may be more effectively promoted through public hearings, which could "reverse" the public condemnation of sentencing by fostering public inclusion within the community (Maruna, 2011). Without dismissing the advantages of closed hearings (e.g., greater privacy and candor), parole hearings ideally should occur under a "presumption of openness" in an open court or other public community settings, as seen in some jurisdictions (e.g., Australia) (Fitzgerald et al., 2023; Hardwick, 2018). This perspective also invites a reconsideration of the formalities surrounding the hearings, such as applicants wearing prison uniforms versus civilian clothing, the board's attire (e.g., robes versus ordinary clothing), and the language used (e.g., legal, clinical, or everyday language), and how these elements might influence parole decision-making. These complex issues warrant further exploration in future studies

Moreover, the way in which the board communicates during hearings requires greater attention. As the findings suggest, the communication of parole rejection by the board often involves stigmatizing and re-censuring messages regarding the applicants' crime and character, effectively becoming a "status rejection" ceremony that denies applicants the opportunity to earn the reformed moral status they believe they deserve (Herbert, 2024; Pogrebin et al., 2015). Thus, policymakers should develop meaningful ways to communicate parole denial without further stigmatizing applicants by implying that their core morality is depraved. After all, as the "Iron Law of Imprisonment" teaches, except for a few, every person we send to prison will eventually return to live with us (Travis, 2005). Thus, even in cases of parole denial, the board's messages should not permanently stain the applicants, prolonging the court's moral condemnation and extending it to society. Overall, the board should convey its decisions to the applicants in non-stigmatizing and ordinary language, recognizing the moral progress they have made (even when the release threshold is not met) and affirming that they are regarded before the law as fellow citizens with moral and social potential rather than merely as risk objects. Additionally, the board should clearly specify what applicants *can* do to improve their chances of parole in the future. This approach could enhance both the moral and reintegrative potential of parole. As with other aspects of parole communication, further research is needed to explore these considerations.

Before concluding, it's important to acknowledge the limitations of the qualitative analysis. The findings may reflect the specific moral labor within a relatively small yet ethnically, socially, and culturally diverse society (Smooha, 2023). Future studies should explore the moral meaning of parole in other socio-legal contexts. Additionally, other interpretations of the data, which may fail to capture the full "unsaid" dynamics during the hearings, are possible (Presser, 2022). Other quantitative (e.g., vignette studies, computational linguistic analysis) and qualitative methods (e.g., ethnography, interviews with various parole legal and correctional actors) could help provide a more complete picture regarding the relations between moral, rational, and emotional considerations (e.g., the relation, if any, between questions of class and race regarding the moral labor used). Such complementary methods should allow us to look beyond a board's post-hoc decision to the real underlying decision-making processes (Dalke & McConnell, 2024). Such methods would also provide the connection, if any, between the moral work relating to the individual case and the wider shared or nonshared ethnic/moral/religious context.

Furthermore, applicants may be incentivized to present a manipulative "parole script" drawing on the experiences of their cellmates or lawyers, and others may feel ashamed to share their feelings openly (Read, 2024; Warr, 2019). It is important to recognize, however, that the potential for concealment, embellishment, or deception is inherent in any form of human communication. Moreover, regardless of the accuracy of the applicants' narratives, they provide valuable insights into what applicants believe is important for their parole, may still influence their own and others' experiences, and can mobilize transformation and recovery (Maruna & Liem, 2021). Furthermore, as positive change is undoubtedly possible for at least some individuals (Maruna & Liem, 2021), dismissing all applicants' narratives as inherently insincere would constitute an "epistemic injustice" toward their voices (Fricker, 2007). Despite these limitations, this study, I hope, provides a much-needed analysis of the hidden moral world of parole. Future research should further examine the moral meaning of other areas within punishment administration theory, policy, and practice.

7 Conclusion

We have come a long way since Adam and Eve's "discovery" of the passage of time. This discovery, as ancient Talmudic masters taught us, allowed them to manage the existential crisis of facing the finality of crime and punishment and the possibility of a second chance. Extending the emerging "moral turn" in criminology to the realm of parole, which motivated this study, sheds light on how modern CJS actors manage this archetypal-existential crisis. Here again, the passage of time was found to be a key factor. Years, possibly decades, after the judge's gavel falls, parole actors engage with moral concerns. Such parole actors revisit justice, and reaffirm, reframe, and sometimes resist the moral meaning of crime, character, and just punishment.

Exploring the moral meaning of parole is important in its own right, and it is my hope that this study will encourage criminologists to broaden the scope of their inquiries to the moral dimensions of other areas within punishment administration. The intensive moral labor found by parole actors in this study should encourage criminologists to further expand this "moral turn" beyond courtrooms. Greater effort should be made to extend the traditional methodological and theoretical boundaries of criminology to explore the less traveled road of morality and punishment administration.

References

Agnew, R. (1992). Foundation for a general strain theory of crime and delinquency. *Criminology*, *30*(1), 47–88.

American Law Institute (ALI) (2017). *Model penal code: Sentencing* (Proposed final draft). Philadelphia.

Anderson, E. (1999). *Code of the street*. Norton.

Andrews, D., & Bonta, J. (2014). *The psychology of criminal conduct* (5th ed.). Routledge.

Annison, H., & Guiney, T. (2022). Populism, conservatism and the politics of parole in England and Wales. *The Political Quarterly*, *93*(3), 416–423.

Appleton, C. (2010). *Life after life imprisonment*. Oxford University Press.

Arrigo, B., & Williams, C. (eds.) (2006). *Philosophy, crime, and criminology*. University of Illinois Press.

Ashworth, A., & Horder, J. (2013). *Principles of criminal law*. Oxford University Press.

Atari, M., Haidt, J., Graham, J., Koleva, S., Stevens, S. T., & Dehghani, M. (2023). Morality beyond the WEIRD: How the nomological network of morality varies across cultures. *Journal of Personality & Social Psychology*, *125*, 1157–1188.

Austin, J. (1979). *Philosophical papers*. Oxford University Press.

Aviram, H. (2020). *Yesterday's monsters: The Manson family cases and the illusion of parole*. University of California Press.

Aviram, H. (2021). Bad role models? American influence on Israeli criminal justice policy. *University of Miami International & Comparative Law Review*, *28*, 309–374.

Avnaim, L. G., & Guetzkow, J. (in press). *Access to justice via parole: Exploring ethno-racial bias and systemic barriers in parole hearings*.

Ball, D. (2011). Normative elements of parole risk. *Stanford Law & Policy Review*, *22*(2), 395–411.

Ball, W. D. (2009). Heinous, Atrocious, and Cruel: "Apprendi", Indeterminate Sentencing, and the Meaning of Punishment. *Columbia Law Review*, 109(5), 893–972.

Bandura, A., Barbaranelli, C., Caprara, G., & Pastorelli, C. (1996). Mechanisms of moral disengagement in the exercise of moral agency. *Journal of Personality & Social Psychology*, *71*(2), 364.

Bartels, D. M., Bauman, C. W., Cushman, F. A., Pizarro, D. A., & McGraw, A. P. (2016). *Moral judgment and decision making*. In G. Keren & G. Wu (Eds.),

The Wiley Blackwell handbook of judgment and decision making (pp. 478–515). Chichester, England: Wiley.

Beard, J. (2023). *The parole system of England and Wales*. House of Commons.

Becker, H. (1963). *Outsiders*. Free Press.

Bibas, S. (2012). *The machinery of criminal justice*. Oxford University Press.

Bing, S. (2011). Reconsidering state parole board membership requirements in light of model penal code sentencing revisions. *Kentucky Law Journal*, 100(3), 871–902.

Bottoms, A. E. (2002). Morality, crime, compliance and public policy. In A. E. Bottoms & M. Tonry (eds.), *Ideology, crime and criminal justice* (pp. 20–51). Willan.

Bottoms, A. E. (2019). Penal censure, repentance and desistance. In A. du Bois-Pedain, & A. E. Bottoms (eds), *Penal censure* (pp. 109–139). Hart.

Bottoms, A. E., & Jacobs, J. (2023). The nature and scope of a moral science. In A. E. Bottoms, & J., Jacobs (eds.), *Criminology as a moral science*. Bloomsbury, pp. 1–50.

Bourdieu, P. (1987). The force of law. *Hastings Law Journal*, 38(5), 814–853.

Bowman, E., & Ely, K. (2017). Examining the predictors of parole release in a rural jail population. *Prison Journal*, 97(5), 543–561.

Brauer, J., & Tittle, C. (2017). When crime is not an option: Inspecting the moral filtering of criminal action alternatives. *Justice Quarterly*, 34(5), 818–846.

Brodeur, J. (1990). The attrition of parole. *Canadian Journal of Criminology*, 32(3), 503–510.

Brookman, F. (2015). The shifting narratives of violent offenders. In L. Presser, & S. Sandberg (eds.), *Narrative Criminology* (pp. 207–234). New York University Press.

Burgess, E. (1936). Protecting the public by parole and by parole prediction. *American Institute of Criminal Law & Criminology*, 27, 491–502.

Calavita, K., & Jenness, V. (2015). *Appealing to justice*. Oakland: University of California Press.

Caplan, J., & Kinnevy, S. (2010). National surveys of state paroling authorities: Models of service delivery. *Federal Probation*, 74, 34–42.

Caplan, J. M. (2012). Protecting parole board legitimacy in the twenty-first century: The role of victims' rights and influences. *Victims & Offenders*, 7(1), 53–76.

Caplan, J. M. (2007). What factors affect parole: A review of empirical research. *Federal Probation: A Journal of Correctional Philosophy and Practice*, 71(1), 16–19.

Charmaz, K. (2006). *Constructing grounded theory*. Sage.

Christie, N. (1977). Conflicts as property. *British Journal of Criminology, 17*(1), 1–15.

Christie, N. (1986). The ideal victim. In I. Anttila (Ed.), *From crime policy to victim policy* (pp. 17–30). London, England: Palgrave Macmillan.

Cochran, J. C., Mears, D. P., Bales, W. D., & Stewart, E. A. (2014). Does inmate behavior affect post-release offending? *Justice Quarterly, 31*(6), 1044–1073.

Cohen, J., Cohen, P., West, S., & Aiken, L. (2013). *Applied multiple regression/correlation analysis for the behavioral sciences*. Routledge.

Cottingham, J. (1979). Varieties of retribution. *The Philosophical Quarterly, 29*(116), 238–246.

Counter-Terrorism Act (2016) (Israel).

Cover, R. (1986). Violence and the word. *Yale Law Journal, 95*, 1601–1629.

Crewe, B., Hulley, S., & Wright, S. (2020). *Life imprisonment from young adulthood*. London: Palgrave Macmillan UK.

Dagan, N., & Rennie, A. (2025). Imagining freedom: Lifers, liberty and the meaning of parole. *Social & Legal Studies*.

Dagan, N. (2022). Exploring the evolution of retributive time through parole decision-making. *British Journal of Criminology, 62*(1), 37–54.

Dagan, N. (2023). Parole as resentencing: Exploring the punitive accounts of parole decision-making through the comparative case study of Israel. *European Journal of Criminology, 20*(4), 1231–1250.

Dagan, N. (2024). Parole as boxing match: Lifers, prosecution, and the adversarial making of parole hearings. *Punishment & Society*, 26(2), 223–242.

Dagan, N., & Roberts, J. V. (2019). Retributivism, penal censure, and life imprisonment without parole. *Criminal Justice Ethics, 38*(1), 1–18.

Dalke, I. (2023). "Insight," compliance, and refurbishing penal practice in California. *Law & Social Inquiry, 48*(1), 1–31.

Dalke, I., & McConnell, B. (2024). The reluctant bureaucrat: Decision-making and justification in shifting legal contexts. https://brendonmcconnell.github.io/pdf/parole_ML.pdf.

Daly, K., & Proietti-Scifoni, G. (2011). Reparation and restoration. In M. Tonry (ed.), *Oxford handbook of crime and criminal justice* (pp. 207–253). Oxford University Press.

Dan-Cohen, M. (1983). Decision rules and conduct rules: On acoustic separation in criminal law. *Harvard Law Review*, 97, 625–677.

Danziger, S., Levav, J., & Avnaim-Pesso, L. (2011). Extraneous factors in judicial decisions. *PNAS, 108*(17), 6889–6892.

de Keijser, J., Roberts, J. V., & Ryberg, J. (2019). Introduction. In J. de Keijser, J. V. Roberts, & J. Ryberg (eds.), *Predictive sentencing* (pp. 1–16). Hart.

Dhami, M. (2016). Effects of a victim's response to an offender's apology. *European Journal of Social Psychology*, *46*(1), 110–123.

DiMaggio, P., & Powell, W. (1983). The iron cage revisited: Institutional isomorphism and collective rationality in organizational fields. *American Sociological Review*, *48*(2), 147–160.

Dobash, R., Dobash, R., Cavanagh, K., & Lewis, R. (2004). Not and ordinary killer – just an ordinary guy: When men murder an intimate woman partner. *Violence Against Women*, *10*, 577–605.

Doe v State (2022). LPA 1981/22 (S.C.) (Israel).

Dorner Report (2015). *The public committee for the review of punishment policy*. Ministry of Justice. www.aac.ac.il/sham/wp-content/uploads/sites/23/2019/07/%D7%93%D7%95%D7%97-%D7%A1%D7%95%D7%A4%D7%99-%D7%97%D7%AA%D7%95%D7%9D-%D7%A0%D7%95%D7%91%D7%9E%D7%91%D7%A8.pdf#page=68.

du Bois-Pedain, A. (2019). Penal desert and the passage of time, In A. du Bois-Pedain & A. E. Bottoms (eds.), *Penal censure* (pp. 227–252). Hart.

du Bois-Pedain, A. (2024). Social rehabilitation as a constitutional principle of justice. In: F. Coppola & A. Martufi (eds.) *Social rehabilitation and criminal justice*, Abingdon: Routledge. pp. 27–52.

Duff, R. A. (2001). *Punishment, communication, and community*. Oxford University Press.

Duff, R. A. (2010). Towards a theory of criminal law? *Aristotelian Society Supplementary*, *84*(1), 1–28.

Durkheim, E. (1893/1997). *The division of labor in society*. Simon & Schuster.

Durkheim, E. (1920/1973). *Emile Durkheim on morality and society*. University of Chicago Press.

Durose, M., Cooper, A., & Snyder, N. (2014). *Recidivism of prisoners released in 30 states in 2005: Patterns from 2005 to 2010* (Vol. 28). Washington, DC: Bureau of Justice Statistics.

Eco, U. (1985). Innovation and repetition: Between modern and post-modern aesthetics. *Daedalus*, *114*, 161–184.

Elo, S., Kääriäinen, M., Kanste, O., Pölkki, T., Utriainen, K., & Kyngäs, H. (2014). Qualitative content analysis: A focus on trustworthiness. *SAGE Open*, *4*(1), 1–10.

Ezeh & Connors v U.K. (2003). (Applications nos. 39665/98 and 40086/98).

Feeley, M., & Simon, J. (1992). The new penology: Notes on the emerging strategy of corrections and its implications. *Criminology*, *30*(4), 449–474.

Fitzgerald, R., Freiberg, A., Dodd, S., & Bartels, L. (2023). *Parole on probation: Parole decision-making, public opinion and public confidence* (Palgrave Socio-Legal Studies). Palgrave Macmillan.

Foucault, M. (1977). *Discipline and punish*. Vintage.

Fricker, M. (2007). *Epistemic injustice*. Oxford University Press.

Ganame v Parole Board (2016). LPA 3340/16 (S.C.) (Israel).

Garland, D. (2001). *The culture of control*. Oxford University Press.

Garland, D. (2011). The problem of the body in modern state punishment. *Social Research*, *78*(3), 767–798.

Gazal-Ayal, O., & Marzuk-Maklada, F. (2023). Administrative release in Israel: When prison capacity determines imprisonment terms. *Tel-Aviv University Law Review*, *47*(1), 57–123 [Hebrew].

Gert, J., & Gert, B. (2025). The definition of morality, *The Stanford Encyclopedia of Philosophy*, E. Zalta & U. Nodelman (eds.), https://plato.stanford.edu/entries/morality-definition/.

Gieryn, T. (1983). Boundary-work and the demarcation of science from non-science: Strains and interests in professional ideologies of scientists. *American Sociological Review*, *48*, 781–795.

Goffman, E. (1959/1980). *The presentation of self in everyday life*. Doubleday.

Goffman, E. (1963/1986). *Stigma: Notes on the management of a spoiled identity*. Simon & Schuster.

Goffman, E. (1971). *Relations in public*. Penguin.

Gottfredson, M., & Hirschi, T. (1990). *A general theory of crime*. Stanford University Press.

Gov (2025). *Parole boards: A guide*. www.gov.il/he/pages/parole_commissions.

Grace, A. (2022). Women's management of the stigma of criminal records. *British Journal of Criminology*, *62*(1), 73–89.

Graham v. Florida 560 U.S. 48 (2010).

Green, B., & Roiphe, R. (2020). When prosecutors politick: Progressive law enforcers then and now. *Journal of Criminal Law & Criminology*, *110*, 719–768.

Greenholtz v Inmates of Nebraska (1979). 442 U.S. 1.

Griffin, B.J., Purcell, N., Burkman, K., Litz, B.T., Bryan, C.J., Schmitz, M., Villierme, C., Walsh, J., & Maguen, S. (2019). Moral injury: An integrative review. *Journal of Traumatic Stress*, *32*(3), 350–362.

Griffin, D. (2018). *Killing time: Life imprisonment and parole in Ireland*. Springer.

Guiney, T. (2023). Parole, parole boards and the institutional dilemmas of contemporary prison release. *Punishment & Society*, *25*(3), 621–640.

Hadar, N., & Gal, T. (2023). Survivors' paths toward forgiveness in restorative justice following sexual violence. *Criminal Justice & Behavior*, *50*(6), 911–928.

Hail-Jares, K. (2021). The impact of non-victim correspondence on parole board decisions. *Justice Quarterly*, *38*(4), 678–700.

Hampton, J. (1984). The moral education theory of punishment. *Philosophy & Public Affairs*, *13*(3), 208–238.

Hanan, M. (2020). Invisible prisons. *UC Davis Law Review*, *54*(3), 1185–1244.

Hannah-Moffat, K. (1999). Moral agent or actuarial subject: Risk and Canadian women's imprisonment. *Theoretical Criminology*, *3*(1), 71–94.

Hannah-Moffat, K. (2013). Actuarial sentencing: An "unsettled" proposition. *Justice Quarterly*, *30*(2), 270–296.

Hardwick, N. (2018). *The work of the parole board*. www.lincolnsinn.org.uk/news/the-work-of-the-parole-board-professor-nick-hardwick/.

Harrison, R., & Duff, R. A. (1988). Punishment and crime. *Proceedings of the Aristotelian Society*, *62*, 139–167.

Haviv, N., Hasisi, B., & Weisburd, D. (2020). Do religious programs in prison work? A quasi-experimental evaluation in the Israeli prison service. *Journal of Experimental Criminology*, *16*(3), 505–533.

Hawkins, K. (1983). Assessing evil-decision behaviour and parole board justice. *British Journal of Criminology*, *23*(2), 101–127.

Herbert, S. (2024). Degradation or redemption? A parole board polices a moral boundary. *Law & Social Inquiry*, *49*(1), 308–328.

Herzog-Evans, M., & Padfield, N. (2015). *The JAP: Lessons for England and Wales*. CJA.

Hoskins, Z. (2014). Ex-offender restrictions. *Journal of Applied Philosophy*, *31*(1), 33–48.

Houser, K. A., Vîlcică, E., Saum, C., & Hiller, M. (2019). Mental health risk factors and parole decisions: Does inmate mental health status affect who gets released. *International Journal of Environmental Research & Public Health*, *16*(16), 2950–2970.

Hritz, A. (2021). Parole board decision-making and constitutional rights. *Annual Review of Law & Social Science*, *17*, 335–351.

Huebner, B., & Bynum, T. (2006). An analysis of parole decision making using a sample of sex offenders: A focal concerns perspective. *Criminology*, *44*(4), 961–991.

Huebner, B., & Bynum, T. (2008). The role of race and ethnicity in parole decisions. *Criminology*, *46*(4), 907–938.

Hulley, S., Crewe, B., & Wright, S. (2016). Re-examining the problems of long-term imprisonment. *British Journal of Criminology*, *56*(4), 769–792.

Ievins, A. (2023). *Moral communication and men convicted of sex offenses*. Oakland: University of California Press.

Ievins, A., & Williams, R. (2025). The moral and ethical worlds of coercive confinement: A prologue. *Incarceration*, *6*, 1–17.

Ignatieff, M. (2000). *The warrior's honor*. Holt.

In re Shaputis, 53 Cal.4th 192 (2011). https://scocal.stanford.edu/opinion/re-shaputis-34046

IPS (2018). *Parole boards*. Israeli Prison Service: Ramla.

IPS (2020). *Annual report for 2019*. Israeli Prison Service: Ramla.

Jaber v State (2017). CA 8328/17 (S.C.) (Israel).

James, V., & Gossett, J. (2018). Of monsters and men: Exploring serial murderers' discourses of neutralization. *Deviant Behavior, 39*(9), 1120–1139.

Jang, S., & Johnson, B. (2024). Religion and rehabilitation as moral reform: Conceptualization and preliminary evidence. *American Journal of Criminal Justice, 49*, 47–73.

Jarman, B. (2020). Only one way to swim? The offence and the life course in accounts of adaptation to life imprisonment. *The British Journal of Criminology, 60*(6), 1460–1479.

Judicial Authority (2023). Parole boards. www.gov.il/he/departments/topics/parole_committees/govil-landing-page.

Kant, I. (1798/1999). *Metaphysical elements of justice*. Hackett.

Kazemian, L., & Travis, J. (2015). Imperative for inclusion of long termers and lifers in research and policy. *Criminology & Public Policy, 14*(2), 355–395.

Kerr, L. (2019). How the prison is a black box in punishment theory. *University of Toronto Law Journal, 69*(1), 85–116.

Kidron, C. A. (2003). Surviving a distant past: A case study of the cultural construction of trauma descendant identity. *Ethos, 31*(4), 513–544.

King, K. (2004). Comparing grieving patterns of the families of murder victims with those of families of death row inmates. *Criminal Justice Policy Review, 15*(2), 193–211.

Kleinstuber, R., & Coldsmith, J. (2020). Is life without parole an effective way to reduce violent crime? An empirical assessment. *Criminology & Public Policy, 19*(2), 617–651.

Krippendorff, K. (2018). *Content Analysis: An Introduction to Its Methodology*. Thousand Oaks, CA: Sage Publications.

Kokkalera, S. S., & Allison, A. M. (2024). The (not so) united states of parole: A state-of-the-art review of discretionary release for individuals serving life. Journal of Criminal Justice and Law, 7(2), 22–41.

Kolber, A. J. (2009). The subjective experience of punishment. Columbia Law Review, 109, 182–236.

Kremnitzer Report (2011). The committee for examining the foundations of homicide offenses. Ministry of Justice [Hebrew] https://fs.knesset.gov.il/%5C20%5CCommittees%5C20_cs_bg_345419.pdf.

Lacey, N. (2016). *In search of criminal responsibility*. Oxford University Press.

Lanskey, C., Markson, L., Souza, K., Ellis, S., Lösel, F., & Barton-Crosby, J. (2023). Morality and motherhood of (ex-)prisoners' Children, in: Bottoms, A. E., Zaibert, L., & Jacobs, J. (Eds.). *Criminology as a moral science*. pp. 127–152. Bloomsbury Publishing.

Larkin Jr, P. J. (2013). Parole: Corpse or phoenix. *American Criminal Law Review*, 50, 303–340.

Laub, J., & Sampson, R. (2003). *Shared beginnings, divergent lives*. Harvard University Press.

Lavin-Loucks, D. (2002). *Building a case and getting out? Inmate strategies for obtaining parole*. PhD dissertation (Indiana University).

Levitt, H. (2021). Qualitative generalization, not to the population but to the phenomenon: Reconceptualizing variation in qualitative research. *Qualitative Psychology*, 8(1), 95–110.

Liebling, A. (2011). Moral performance, inhuman and degrading treatment and prison pain. *Punishment & Society*, 13(5), 530–550.

Liebling, A. (2021). What is philosophy in prison? George Eliot and the search for moral insight. *Journal of Prison Education & Reentry*, 7(2), 104–114.

Liem, M., & Richardson, N. (2014). The role of transformation narratives in desistance among released lifers. *Criminal Justice & Behavior*, 41(6), 692–712.

Lin, J., Grattet, R., & Petersilia, J. (2010). "Back-end sentencing" and reimprisonment: Individual, organizational, and community predictors of parole sanctioning decisions. *Criminology*, 48(3), 759–795.

Locke, J. (1690/1988). *Two treatises of government*. Cambridge University Press.

Lynch, M. (1998). Waste managers? The new penology, crime fighting, and parole agent identity. *Law & Society Review*, 32(4), 839–870.

Makkai, T., & Braithwaite, J. (1994). Reintegrative shaming and compliance with regulatory standards. *Criminology*, 32(3), 361–385.

Martin, R. (2024). *Sentencing for murder: A Review of Policy and Practice*. Sentencing Academy. www.sentencingacademy.org.uk/wp-content/uploads/2024/04/Sentencing-for-Murder-A-Review-of-Policy-and-Practice.pdf.

Maruna, S. (2011). Reentry as a rite of passage. *Punishment & Society*, 13(1), 3–28.

Maruna, S., & Copes, H. (2005). What have we learned from five decades of neutralization research? *Crime & Justice*, 32, 221–320.

Maruna, S., & Liem, M. (2021). Where is this story going? A critical analysis of the emerging field of narrative criminology. *Annual Review of Criminology*, 4, 125–146.

Maruna, S., & Mann, R. (2006). A fundamental attribution error? Rethinking cognitive distortions. *Legal & Criminological Psychology*, 11(2), 155–177.

Maruna, S. (2001). *Making good: How ex-convicts reform and reclaim their lives*. Washington, DC: American Psychological Association.

Maslen, H. (2015). *Remorse, penal theory and sentencing*. Hart.

Matejkowski, J., Draine, J., Solomon, P., & Salzer, M. (2011). Mental illness, criminal risk factors and parole release decisions. *Behavioral Sciences & the Law*, *29*(4), 528–553.

Matiošaitis and others v. Lithuania (2017). ECHR (nos. 22662/13 and others).

Matza, D. (1964). *Delinquency and drift*. Wiley.

Maurutto, P., & Hannah-Moffat, K. (2006). Assembling risk and the restructuring of penal control. *British Journal of Criminology*, *46*(3), 438–454.

May, H. (1999). Who killed whom? Victimization and culpability in the social construction of murder. *British Journal of Sociology*, *50*(3), 489–506.

McFadden, P. (1987). The balancing test. *Boston College Law Review*, *29*, 585–656.

McNeill, F. (2012). Four forms of "offender" rehabilitation: Towards an interdisciplinary perspective. *Legal & Criminological Psychology*, *17*(1), 18–36.

McNeill, F., Burns, N., Halliday, S., Hutton, N., & Tata, C. (2009). Risk, responsibility and reconfiguration: Penal adaptation and misadaptation. *Punishment & Society*, *11*(4), 419–442.

McNeill, F., & Maruna, S. (2010). Paying back and trading up: Reforming character. Presented at the European Society of Criminology Conference, Liege.

Medwed, D. (2008). The innocent prisoner's dilemma: Consequences of failing to admit guilt at parole hearings. *Iowa Law Review*, *93*(2), 491–557.

Messner, S. (2012). Morality, markets, and the ASC: 2011 presidential address to the American Society of Criminology. *Criminology*, *50*(1), 5–25.

Meyers, D. (2016). *Victims' stories and the advancement of human rights*. Oxford University Press.

Miller v. Alabama, 567 U.S. 460 (2012).

Millie, A. (2016). *Philosophical criminology*. Policy Press.

Ministry of Justice (2022). *Root and branch review of the parole system*. https://assets.publishing.service.gov.uk/media/624438e8e90e075f1120586a/root-branch-review-parole-system.pdf.

Mitchell, B., & Roberts, J. V. (2012). *Exploring the mandatory life sentence for murder*. Bloomsbury.

Mooney, J., & Daffern, M. (2014). Elucidating the factors that influence parole decision-making and violent offenders' performance on parole. *Psychiatry, Psychology & Law*, *21*(3), 385–405.

Moore, J. (2011). Alexander Maconochie's 'mark system'. *Prison Service Journal*, *198*, 38–46.

Morgan, K. & Smith, B. (2005). Victims, punishment, and parole: The effect of victim participation on parole hearings. *Criminology & Public Policy*, 4(2), 333–360.

Morris, N. (1974). *The Future of Imprisonment*. Chicago: University of Chicago Press.

Morris, N. (2003). *The story of Norfolk Island and the roots of modern prison reform*. Oxford University Press.

Murcia, E. (2022). Prosecutors, parole, and evidence: Why excluding prosecutors from parole hearings will improve California's parole process. *Loyola Law Review*, 55(2), 441–476.

Murphy, J., & Hampton, J. (1988). *Forgiveness and mercy*. Cambridge University Press.

Murphy, J. G. (2012). Punishment and moral emotions: Essays in law, morality, and religion. New York: Oxford.

Na'Aman, O. (2020). The fitting resolution of anger. *Philosophical Studies*, 177(8), 2417–2430.

Nagel, I. H. (1990). Foreword: Structuring sentencing discretion: The new federal sentencing guidelines. *The Journal of Criminal Law and Criminology*, 80(4), 883–943.

Nellis, A., & Bishop, T. (2021). A new lease for life. The Sentencing Project. www.sentencingproject.org/app/uploads/2022/08/A-New-Lease-on-Life.pdf.

New-York State Parole Handbook (2010). http://newyorkparolelawyer.com/parolehandbook.pdf (last accessed 8 June 2025).

Ostermann, M. (2015). How do former inmates perform in the community? A survival analysis of rearrests, reconvictions, and technical parole violations. *Crime & Delinquency*, 61(2), 163–187.

Ouaknine, Y., Ben-Zvi, K., & Carmel, T. (2021). The impact of the corrective rehabilitative program on the parole board's decisions. *Prison Service Journal*, 21, 148–165 [Hebrew].

Padfield, N., Annison, M. J., Calvert-Smith, D., Conway, M., Creighton, S., Herbert, R., Janes, L., Karve, C., Kider, S., Kingham, D. and Latham, D., (2023). *A parole system fit for purpose*. London, Justice.

Padfield, N., Liebling, A., & Arnold, H. (2000). *An exploration of decision-making at discretionary lifer panels*. Home Office.

Padfield, N., van Zyl Smit, D., & Dünkel, F. (eds.). (2010). *Release from prison*. Routledge.

Padfield, N. (2025). Victims at parole, in: M. Manikis & G. Watson (eds), Sentencing, Public Opinion, and Criminal Justice: Essays in Honour of Julian V Roberts, Oxford University Press. pp. 265–273.

Palacios, V. (1994). Go and sin no more: Rationality and release decisions by parole boards. *South Carolina Law Review*, 45, 567–615.

Palmor Report. (2010). Parole boards examination report. Ministry of Justice, Jerusalem. [Hebrew].

Paparozzi, M., & Caplan, J. (2009). A profile of paroling authorities in America: The strange bedfellows of politics and professionalism. *Prison Journal*, 89(4), 401–425.

Parole Board (2022). *The parole board decision-making framework*. https://assets.publishing.service.gov.uk/media/63906a7d8fa8f569f4902091/Decision_Making_Framework_Guidance_version_1.2_-_external_version.pdf.

Parole Law (2001). (Israel).

Parole Procedures (2025). Interministerial regulation. www.gov.il/BlobFolder/policy/interministerial_regulation_12_001_20/he/%D7%A0%D7%95%D7%94%D7%9C%20%D7%95%D7%A2%D7%93%D7%95%D7%AA%20%D7%A9%D7%97%D7%A8%D7%95%D7%A8%D7%99%D7%9D%20-%20%D7%AA%D7%99%D7%A7%D7%95%D7%9F%20%D7%9E%D7%A1'%206-%20%D7%A4%D7%91%D7%A8%D7%95%D7%90%D7%A8%202025%20-%20%D7%A1%D7%95%D7%A4%D7%99.pdf.

PCATI v Parole Board (2001). HCJ 89/01 (S.C) (Israel).

Pedan, E. (2019). Israeli state attorney's office 3. *Tel-Aviv University Journal of Law & Social Change*, 13, 411–448.

Penal Code Bill (Amendment No. 119) (Offenses of Murder), 2015.

Penal Law, 1977 [2019] (amendment no. 137) (Israel).

Petersilia, J. (2003). *Parole and prisoner reentry*. Oxford University Press.

Piquero, A. (2017). "No remorse, no repent": Linking lack of remorse to criminal offending in a sample of serious adolescent offenders. *Justice Quarterly*, 34(2), 350–376.

Pogrebin, M. R., Stretesky, P. B., Walker, A., & Opsal, T. (2015). Rejection, humiliation, and parole: A study of parolees' perspectives. *Symbolic Interaction*, 38(3), 413–430.

Presser, L. (2022). *Unsaid: Analyzing harmful silences*. Oakland: University of California Press.

Prison Service Order (PSO) (2011). PSO 4700. MOJ.

Prison Rehabilitation Authority (2022). Vision and purpose. https://www.gov.il/he/pages/01vision_and_goals.

Proctor, J. L. (1999). The "new parole": An analysis of parole board decision making as a function of eligibility. *Journal of Crime and Justice*, 22(2), 193–217.

Proeve, M. (2023). Addressing the challenges of remorse in the criminal justice system. *Psychiatry, Psychology & Law*, 30(1), 68–82.

Read, B. (2024). The parole dossier and its negative impacts on prisoner identity. *Criminology & Criminal Justice*.

Reitz, K. (2017). *The question of parole release authority: Reporter's study*, ALI: PA.

Reitz, K., & Rhine, E. (2020). Parole release and supervision: Critical drivers of American prison policy. *Annual Review of Criminology*, 3(1), 281–298.

Rhine, E., Petersilia, J., & Reitz, K. (2017). The future of parole release. *Crime & Justice*, 46(1), 279–338.

Riches, G., & Dawson, P. (1998). Spoiled memories: Problems of grief resolution in families bereaved by murder. *Mortality*, 3(2), 143–159.

Rieger, D., & Serin, R. (2024). Parole decision-making and empirical practice. *Prison Journal*, 104(1), 46–67.

Rights of Victims of Crime Law (2001) (Israel).

Rivera-Laugalis, V., Kokkalera, S., & Wronski, B. (2024). Examining parole decision-making pre-and post-COVID-19. *Criminal Justice & Behavior*, 51(11), 1715–1733.

Roberts, J. V., & Gazal-Ayal, O. (2013). Statutory sentencing reform in Israel: Exploring the sentencing law of 2012. *Israel Law Review*, 46(3), 455–479.

Roberts, J. V., & Maslen, H. (2014). After the crime: Retributivism, post-offence conduct and penal censure. In A. Simester, A. du Bois-Pedain, & U. Neumann (eds.), *Liberal Criminal Theory: Essays for Andreas von Hirsch* (pp. 88–109). Hart.

Roberts, J. V., & Erez, E. (2004). Communication in sentencing: Exploring the expressive function of victim impact statements. *International Review of Victimology*, 10(3), 223–244.

Roberts, J. V., & Gazal-Ayal, O. (2013). Statutory sentencing reform in Israel: Exploring the sentencing law of 2012. *Israel Law Review*, 46(3), 455–479.

Roberts, J. V., Nuffield, J., & Hann, R. (2000). *Parole and the public: Attitudinal and behavioural responses*. University of Ottawa.

Roberts, J. V. (2008). Punishing persistence: explaining the enduring appeal of the recidivist sentencing premium. *The British Journal of Criminology*, 48(4), 468–481.

Robinson, P. (2012). Life without parole under modern theories of punishment. In C. Ogletree & A. Sarat (eds.), *Life without parole: America's new death penalty?* (pp. 138–166). New York University.

Robinson, P., & Holcomb, L. (2021). The criminogenic effects of damaging criminal law's moral credibility. *Southern California Interdisciplinary Law Journal*, 31, 277–327.

Roberts, J. V. (2008). Punishing persistence: explaining the enduring appeal of the recidivist sentencing premium. *The British Journal of Criminology*, 48(4), 468–481.

Rock, P. (1998). Murderers, victims and "survivors" The Social Construction of Deviance. *The British Journal of Criminology, 38*(2), 185–200.

Rosenfeld, M., & Noah, R. (2021). (No)-parole committees? An empirical study of parole in Israel. *The Hebrew University Journal of Legislation, 15*, 9–66 [Hebrew].

Rotman, E. (2024). The history of rehabilitation as a penological principle. In F. Coppola, & A. Martufi (eds.), *Social rehabilitation and criminal justice* (pp. 13–26). Routledge.

Rubin, E. (2003). Just say no to retribution. *Buffalo Criminal Law Review, 7*, 17–83.

Ruhland, E. (2020). Philosophies and decision making in parole board members. *Prison Journal, 100*, 640–661.

Ruhland, E. L., Rhine, E. E., Robey, J. P., & Mitchell, K. L. (2017). *The continuing leverage of releasing authorities*. Robina Institute of Criminal Law and Criminal Justice, University of Minnesota.

Ruhland, E., & Laskorunsky, J. (2025). The hearing is just a formality: You're never getting out. *Crime & Delinquency, 71*(1), 248–271.

Ryberg, J. (2025). Sentencing offenders the right way: On the importance of relating penal theory and penal practice. *Criminal Law Forum, 36*, 191–204.

Schinkel, M. (2014). Punishment as moral communication. *Punishment & Society, 16*(5), 578–597.

Seeds, C. (2022). *Death by prison: Emergence of life without parole and perpetual confinement*. University of California Press.

Shammas, V. (2019). California lifers, performative dialogue, and the ideology of insight. *Political & Legal Anthropology Review, 42*(2), 142–160.

Sharon, E. (2003). *Early release from prison*. Nevo [Hebrew].

Sharpe, S. (2013). The idea of reparation. In G. Johnstone & D. Van Ness (eds.), *Handbook of restorative justice* (pp. 24–40). Willan.

Shute, D. (2004). Does parole work? The empirical evidence from England and Wales. *Ohio State Journal of Criminal Law, 2*, 315–331.

Simon, J. (1993). *Poor discipline*. University of Chicago Press.

Skipper v South Carolina 476 US 1 (1986).

Slobogin, C., & Brinkley-Rubinstein, L. (2013). Putting desert in its place. *Stanford Law Review, 65*, 77–135.

Smith, N. (2016). Dialectical retributivism. *Philosophia, 44*(2), 343–360.

Smooha, S. (2023). Ethnic and cultural diversity in Israeli society. In K. Fraiman, & D. Phillip-Bell (eds.), *The Routledge handbook of Judaism in the 21st century* (pp. 68–88). Routledge.

Snacken, S. (2021). Human dignity and prisoners' rights in Europe. *Crime and Justice: A Review of Research, 50*(1), 301–351.

Solomon, A., Kachnowski, V., & Bhati, A. (2005). *Does parole work? Analyzing the impact of postprison supervision on re-arrest outcomes*. Washington, DC: Urban Institute.

State Attorney (2018). *The prosecution committee for examining the application of the Dorner Report*. Ministry of Justice.

State v Ganame (2009). LPA 10349/08 (S.C.) (Israel).

Stazenko v State (2018). LPA 3749/17 (S.C.) (Israel).

Stygall, G. (2012). Discourse in the US courtroom. In P. Tiersma, & L. Solan (eds.), *The Oxford Handbook of language and law* (pp. 369–380). Oxford University Press.

Sykes, G., & Matza, D. (1957). Techniques of neutralization: A theory of delinquency. *American Sociological Review, 22*(6), 664–670.

Tadros, V. (2011). *The ends of harm: The moral foundations of criminal law*. Oxford University Press.

Tangney, J., Stuewig, J., & Hafez, L. (2011). Shame, guilt, and remorse: Implications for offender populations. *Journal of Forensic Psychiatry & Psychology, 22*(5), 706–723.

Tangney, J. P., Stuewig, J., & Martinez, A. G. (2014). Two faces of shame: The roles of shame and guilt in predicting recidivism. *Psychological Science, 25*(3), 799–805.

The Sentencing Project. (2024). *The second look movement*. www.sentencingproject.org.

Tractate Avodah-Zarah (2020). The William Davidson edition. www.sefaria.org/Avodah_Zarah?tab=contents.

Travis, J. (2005). *But they all come back: Facing the challenges of prisoner reentry*. The Urban Institute.

Tyler, T. (2010). Legitimacy in corrections: Policy implications. *Criminology & Public Policy, 9*(1), 127–134.

UK Parole Board (2015). *Information for victims*. https://assets.publishing.service.gov.uk/media/5a749113ed915d0e8e3993ae/Parole_Board_-_Information_for_Victims.pdf.

Van Ginneken, E., & Hayes, D. (2017). "Just" punishment? Offenders' views on the meaning and severity of punishment. *Criminology & Criminal Justice, 17*(1), 62–78.

van Zyl Smit, D., & Appleton, C. (2019). *Life imprisonment: A global human rights analysis*. Harvard University Press.

van Zyl Smit, D., & Corda, A. (2018). American exceptionalism in parole release and supervision. In K. Reitz (ed.), *American exceptionalism in crime and punishment* (pp. 410–486). Oxford University Press.

Victims' Commissioner (2024). *What to expect from the justice system*. https://victimscommissioner.org.uk/victims/help-for-victims/parole/.

Vîlcică, E. (2018). Testing for the punitive hypothesis in a large US jurisdiction. *International Journal of Offender Therapy & Comparative Criminology, 62* (5), 1357–1383.

Vinter v U.K. (2013) ECHR (Applications nos. 66069/09, 130/10 and 3896/10).

von Hirsch, A. (2017). *Deserved criminal sentences*. Hart.

von Hirsch, A & Ashworth. A. (2005). *Proportionate sentencing: Exploring the principles*. Oxford, U.K.: Oxford University Press.

von Hirsch, A., & Hanrahan, K. (1978). *Abolish parole?* Washington, DC: U.S. Government Printing Office.

Walk, D., & Dagan, N. (2024). Rehabilitation vs. risk: What predicts parole board decisions and rehabilitation authority recommendations?. *Punishment & Society, 26*(5), 769–789.

Warr, J. (2019). Lifers, risk, rehabilitation, and narrative labour. *Punishment & Society, 22*(1), 28–47.

Weinshall, K. (2024). Reconceptualizing judicial activism: intervention versus involvement in the Israeli supreme court. *Journal of Law & Empirical Analysis, 1*(2), 343–357.

Weisburd, D., Ariel, B., Braga, A.A., Eck, J., Gill, C., Groff, E., Uding, C.V., & Zaatut, A. (2025). The future of the criminology of place: New directions for research and practice. In Weisburd, D. (ed.), *Elements in Criminology*, pp. 1–110. Cambridge University Press.

Weisman, R. (2009). The judicial use of remorse to construct character and community. *Social & Legal Studies, 18*(1), 47–69.

Werth, R. (2017). Moral judgement, professional knowledge and affect in parole evaluations. *British Journal of Criminology, 57*(4), 808–827.

Whitman, J. (2014). The case for penal modernism. *Critical Analysis of Law, 1* (2), 143–181.

Young, K., & Chimowitz, H. (2022). How parole boards judge remorse. *Law & Society Review, 56*(2), 237–260.

Young, K., & Pearlman, J. (2022). Racial disparities in lifer parole outcomes: The hidden role of professional evaluations. *Law & Social Inquiry, 47*(3), 783–820.

Young, K., Mukamal, D., & Favre-Bulee, T. (2016). Predicting parole grants: An analysis of suitability hearings for California's lifer inmates. *Federal Sentencing Reporter, 28*(4), 268–277.

Acknowledgments

I wish to acknowledge with gratitude the contributions of mentors, colleagues, and institutions that have guided and supported this research.

David Weisburd provided mentorship that shaped this manuscript from its inception to completion. During my doctoral studies, Ruth Kannai, and during my postdoctoral research, Julian V. Roberts, planted the intellectual seeds for this work more than a decade ago.

Marion Vannier generously offered thoughtful commentary on the manuscript, and Irit Ballas provided insights that strengthened the study's proposal. Adiel Zimran and Shmuel Baron assisted in refining the normative analysis. I also benefited from intellectual exchanges with Hadar Dancig-Rosenberg, Ben Jarman, and Ailie Rennie.

The statistical analysis was enriched by the expert advice of Roni Factor, Naomi Kaplan-Damary, and Shlomit Weiss-Dagan. I am particularly indebted to Maria Trotsky for her excellent assistance with the data analysis.

Yochi Sochatzevski, Liat Dreyer, and Yuli Bauman provided valuable research assistance. Eve Horowitz-Leibowitz enhanced the clarity and precision of the manuscript.

I am grateful to Rotem Efodi-Sha'ar and Dror Walk of the Prison Rehabilitation Authority, whose unwavering support facilitated crucial data access.

The Institute for Criminology at the Hebrew University provided an exceptional academic environment conducive to criminological scholarship.

This research was supported by the Israel Science Foundation (grant No. 2524/24).

Finally, I thank my parents, Avraham and Rivka Dagan, as well as my wife, Shlomit, and our children Neta, Kerem, and Zohar, for their love and support.

Criminology

David Weisburd
George Mason University, Virginia
Hebrew University of Jerusalem

Advisory Board

Professor Catrien Bijleveld, *VU University Amsterdam*
Professor Francis Cullen, *University of Cincinnati*
Professor Manuel Eisner, *Cambridge University*
Professor Elizabeth Groff, *Temple University*
Professor Cynthia Lum, *George Mason University*
Professor Lorraine Mazerolle, *University of Queensland*
Professor Daniel Nagin, *Carnegie Mellon University*
Professor Ojmarrh Mitchell, *University of California, Irvine*
Professor Alex Piquero, *University of Miami*
Professor Richard Rosenfeld, *University of Missouri*

About the Series

Elements in Criminology seeks to identify key contributions in theory and empirical research that help to identify, enable, and stake out advances in contemporary criminology. The series focuses on radical new ways of understanding and framing criminology, whether of place, communities, persons, or situations. The relevance of criminology for preventing and controlling crime is also be a key focus of this series.

Cambridge Elements

Criminology

Elements in the Series

Confronting School Violence: A Synthesis of Six Decades of Research
Jillian J. Turanovic, Travis C. Pratt, Teresa C. Kulig and Francis T. Cullen

Testing Criminal Career Theories in British and American Longitudinal Studies
John F. MacLeod and David P. Farrington

Legitimacy-Based Policing and the Promotion of Community Vitality
Tom Tyler and Caroline Nobo

Making Sense of Youth Crime: A Comparison of Police Intelligence in the United States and France
Jacqueline E. Ross and Thierry Delpeuch

Toward a Criminology of Terrorism
Gary LaFree

Using the Police Craft to Improve Patrol Officer Decision-Making
James J. Willis and Heather Toronjo

Crime Dynamics: Why Crime Rates Change Over Time
Richard Rosenfeld

Partnerships in Policing: How Third Parties Help Police to Reduce Crime and Disorder
Lorraine Mazerolle, Kevin Petersen, Michelle Sydes and Janet Ransley

The Future of the Criminology of Place: New Directions for Research and Practice
David Weisburd, Barak Ariel, Anthony A. Braga, John Eck, Charlotte Gill, Elizabeth Groff, Clair V. Uding and Amarat Zaatut

The Hidden Measurement Crisis in Criminology: Procedural Justice as a Case Study
Amanda Graham, Francis T. Cullen and Bruce G. Link

Beyond Traditional Conceptions of Policing and Crime Control: New Metrics to Evaluate Police Performance and Improve Police Legitimacy
Dennis P. Rosenbaum

Revisiting Justice: The Moral Meaning of Parole
Netanel Dagan

A full series listing is available at: www.cambridge.org/ECRM

For EU product safety concerns, contact us at Calle de José Abascal, 56–1°,
28003 Madrid, Spain or eugpsr@cambridge.org.

www.ingramcontent.com/pod-product-compliance
Lightning Source LLC
LaVergne TN
LVHW011848060526
838200LV00054B/4225